FORTRESS OF MY YOUTH

Memoir of a Terezín Survivor

JANA RENÉE FRIESOVÁ

Translated by
Elinor Morrisby and Ladislav Rosendorf

THE UNIVERSITY OF WISCONSIN PRESS

The University of Wisconsin Press
1930 Monroe Street, 3rd floor
Madison, Wisconsin 53711-2059
uwpress.wisc.edu

3 Henrietta Street
London WC2E 8LU, England
eurospanbookstore.com

Printed in the United States of America

Library of Congress Cataloging-in-Publication Data

Friesová, Jana Renée, 1927–
    [Pevnost mého mládí. English]
    Fortress of my youth : memoir of a Terezín survivor / Jana Renée Friesová;
    translated by Elinor Morrisby and Ladislav Rosendorf.
        pp.   cm.
    ISBN 0-299-17810-2 (cloth : alk. paper)
    1. Friesová, Jana Renée, 1927– 2. Jews—Persecutions—Czech Republic—Prague.
3. Holocaust, Jewish (1939–1945)—Czech Republic—Prague—Personal narratives.
4. Prague (Czech Republic)—Ethnic relations. 5. Theresienstadt (Concentration camp)
I. Title.
DS135.C96 P718913   2002
940.53'18'092—dc21   2001052471

ISBN-13: 978-0-299-17814-7 (pbk: alk. paper)

Jana Renée Friesová was born in Prague in 1927. She was deported to the Terezín ghetto in 1942. After the war she resumed her studies and completed a PhD at the Charles University, Prague, in 1952. She taught philosophy and aesthetics at the University until her retirement in 1979. Renée Friesová lives in Prague, teaches yoga, works as a counsellor and recently lectured in Jewish Studies at the Charles University. She has translated works by Kazantzakis from English to Czech and, more recently, work by Judy Blume, the children's writer. She has also travelled extensively throughout Europe, Australia, Canada and the United States. She has made a video recording of her experiences as a Holocaust survivor and is currently working for the Shoah Foundation in Prague.

To my daughter Lenka and her children, Hannah, Rachel, and Benjamin, as well as to my son-in-law, Rubin, my husband, Ota Gregor, and to Elinor, my closest friend.

Principal Translator's Note

I first met Renée Friesová in 1969, the year in which I began studies in music at the Prague Conservatorium. Twenty-seven years later, I am honoured to be able to translate her book into English.

I wish to record warm thanks to my fellow translator Ladislav Rosendorf, whose commitment, time and patience have been an integral part of this translation.

The Czech version of names and places has been retained throughout the book, with the obvious exceptions of Prague (Praha) and Auschwitz. Some personal names in the book retain the variant forms that apply in Czech. For example, the wife and daughter of Richard Fries were known by the feminine surname Friesová. Similarly the Czech use of affectionate diminutives allows a name such as Jarmila to appear in any intimate context as Jarmilka.

Hobart, Tasmania,
Australia
November 1995

Contents

Dates of significant events

1938

30 September   The Munich Agreement, signed by Hitler, Chamberlain, Daladier and Mussolini, forced Czechoslovakia to give up the Sudeten Land. Nazi Germany took over one-fifth of Czechoslovakian territory.

1939

15 March   The German army entered Prague. The Protectorate of Bohemia and Moravia was established. Up until that time Jewish children attended state schools.

26 July   The *Zentralstelle für Auswanderung der Juden* (Centre for Jewish Emigration) was set up. Immediately, a census of the Jewish population was carried out.

1 December   Jewish children were expelled from state schools.

1940

14 June   The concentration camp at Auschwitz was established.

1941

27 September   Reinhard Heydrich was named as Head of the Protectorate in Czechoslovakia. One of his first acts was to order the mass deportation of Jews and the conversion of the small town of Terezín into a Jewish ghetto.

16 October   The first transport left Prague for the ghetto at Lodz. It included children.

24 November   The first transport of Jews arrived at Terezín.

1942

9 January to 26 October	Transports from Terezín to the east began, with an average of 1,000 people in each one. Children were included in these transports. Of the people taken, only one per cent ever returned.
3 June	Heydrich was assassinated by means of a bomb, in Prague.
31 August	There were now 51,554 inmates in Terezín. Each person had a 1.6 square metre floor-space. The average working time was 80–100 hours per week. Children aged 14 and over had the same work responsibilities as the adults. Between 106 and 156 people died daily.
18 September	There were 58,497 prisoners in Terezín.
6 December	There were 3,541 children living in Terezín. Approximately 2,000 of them lived in designated Children's Homes.

1943

31 December	There were 3,031 children in Terezín, 1,969 of them in the Children's Homes.

1944

31 December	Only 819 children up to the age of 15 were accounted for in Terezín.

1945

7 May	Terezín was liberated by Russian troops.

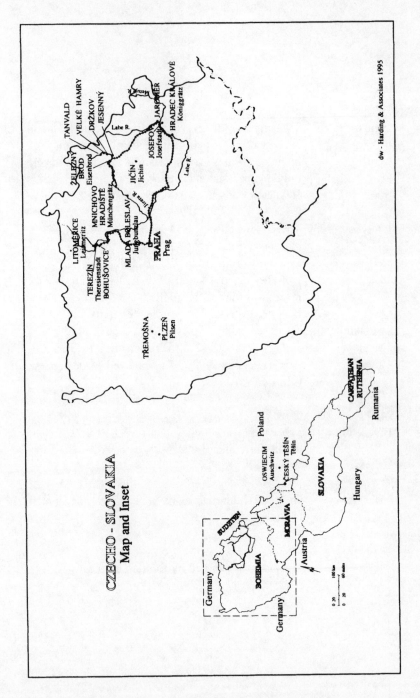

CZECHO - SLOVAKIA
Map and Inset

dw - Harding & Associates 1995

TŘEMOŠNÁ

PLZEŇ
Pilsen

LITOMĚŘICE
Leitmeritz

TEREZÍN
Theresienstadt
BOHUŠOVICE

MNICHOVO
HRADIŠTĚ
Münchengrätz

MLADÁ BOLESLAV
Jungbunzlau

ŽELEZNÝ
BROD
Eisenbrod

TANVALD

VELKÉ HAMRY

DRŽKOV

JESENNÝ

JIČÍN
Jičin

PRAHA
Prag

JOSEFOV
Josefstadt

JAROMĚŘ

HRADEC KRÁLOVÉ
Königgrätz

Metuje R.

Labe R.

Labe R.

Jizera R.

Germany

Germany

Austria

BOHEMIA

SUDETEN

MORAVIA

OSWIECIM
Auschwitz

ČESKÝ TĚŠÍN
Těšín

Poland

SLOVAKIA

Hungary

CARPATHIAN
RUTHENIA

Rumania

0   20   100 km
0   20   60 miles

x

Prelude

Between dreaming and being awake, I am the master of time. Nothing matters – the year, the hour, the day of the week, or even the weather. I am where I want to be, I see what I want to see. I alone dictate my setting. People come and go, things appear and disappear. There are even moments when it seems that the shadows of my dead ones will never return and that they have disappeared forever. That is an unbearable feeling. So I slide back into sleep and await the touch of those no longer living. They are kind, yet they still come back to live with, and within, me.

Only in the limitless greyness of day does reality emerge. The present forces itself upon me and tries to blanket the memories of my beloved dead. Prayers for the dead, the silent Kaddish – the Hebrew prayer, mourning a deceased relative year after year – and pebbles on the graves of strangers are all that remain. My loved ones are far away in time and place. Yes, there are books and movies about this twentieth-century apocalypse, more and more of them, but they are hardly sufficient for the incredible suffering inflicted. What remain are good or bad books, better or worse films. There is no one who resembles my dear ones among the actors who portray those inhumanly sentenced to death. My pain is my tie with the past, and you can touch that pain, so that everything that has happened in this century of 'progress' must be believed.

Only between dreaming and being awake am I the master of time.

*

In 1941 the Nazis decided to resolve 'the Jewish question' once and for all. In this so-called final solution, the Bohemian town of Terezín (Theresienstadt), 60 kilometres north of Prague, played a significant part. A fortress built in Maria Theresa's time, it had had to wait until the twentieth century to fulfil its historical role. This small town of barracks and crisscrossing streets, seemingly designed by set-square on an Austrian aichitect's drawing-board, was to become a ghetto. The town was turned into a concentration camp, a show-piece for the world to see how well the German Empire looked after the Jews.

About 5,000 residents were moved out and the barracks were emptied. The first transport of Jews arrived in Terezín on 24 November 1941. The first two transports, numbered AK 1 and AK 2 (AK standing for *Aufbau Komando*, Building Commando), brought 342 young Jewish men to prepare the town, with its already minimal sanitary facilities, for the arrival of tens of thousands of people.

During the three-and-a-half years of war when it was a ghetto, the number of people in Terezín varied between 30,000 and 60,000. In the weeks or months when the ghetto held 'only' 30,000 people, each person had 3.5 square metres of space, including the area of the streets, in which to move. These conditions unremittingly influenced the mental and physical state of the prisoners.

The Germans decided that the Terezín ghetto would be self-governing. This was a fiendishly neat solution, as it made a Jewish Council responsible for compiling lists for the transports to 'the east'.

All the fundamental laws regulating prison life were formulated by the Germans. There were, for example, these two regulations:

§ 8. The smuggling of letters is punishable by death. Any attempt will be judged as the completed act itself.

§ 10. Illegal departure from the ghetto is considered to be an attempt at escape. The guards are empowered to use firearms to prevent such attempts.

Ramparts, gates, guards and wire separated this ghetto town from the rest of occupied Bohemia.

Scenes from childhood

In 1937, when I was ten, my mother gave me an autograph book. In 1942, just before we were forced to leave our home, I entrusted this book to a school friend who lived in our house. After the war she returned it to me. The sayings in it are precocious, sweet and a little ridiculous, as in all girls' autograph books. But those were serious times, so it was not by chance that one of my teachers, Jaroslava Lieblová, wrote for me in June 1940 'In your lifetime, if you are ever laden with burdens that fate has put in your path, conjure up the heavenly memories of childhood and believe that you can overcome even the most cruel misfortune.'

I cannot remember Mrs Lieblová's face, but I can guarantee that she was right. Recalling my childhood always helped me endure the seemingly unendurable.

My step-grandfather, Jan Sieger, a judge in the small town of Mnichovo Hradiště, was not a Jew. Grandmother Františka, née Fantová, loved him and married him after the death in 1914 of her first husband Adolf Bondy, who was my real grandfather. Adolf Bondy had been conscripted into the Austro-Hungarian Imperial army, but on the way to the barracks he died of a heart attack. It was suggested that there had been an affair between Grandmother and Jan Sieger while she was still married to Adolf, but it was a taboo subject around

3

which everyone moved very carefully. Jan certainly behaved as a loving father towards my mother and her brother. No one will ever know the truth and, anyway, it is not important.

According to the Nuremberg Laws, anti-Jewish decrees introduced in 1935 by the Nazi government, Grandfather Sieger was an Aryan. His ancestors' origins were 'suitable', unlike Grandmother's and those of Grandfather Bondy. I only know that Grandpa Sieger's father was a blacksmith in the village of Třemošná, near Plzeň.

A deep affection existed between Grandpa and myself. He used to improvise on the piano and I used to dance. He had studied in Plzeň and was an excellent musician, a fine pianist and singer. As a guest singer in the Plzeň Opera he had sung Lohengrin, and I often day-dreamed while looking at the photograph in which the hero is carried away by swans. This first hero of my childhood was also a member of one of the first skiing clubs in Bohemia. He competed in the Ještěd mountain downhill race using one long pole as a brake between the skis. He was also one of the first people in Plzeň to own a car. Later, he tried flying in a biplane with Františka, my grandmother.

Grandpa genuinely embraced nature, from the ground to the heavens. He taught me about flowers, rocks, birds and stars. Today, I am convinced he was a pantheist. He recalled the disputes about Catholic dogma that he had had with a priest, his teacher of religious instruction at the Royal College, which led to the only bad mark in his matriculation results. When he was approaching sixty he still hadn't forgiven that teacher. In spite of this, however, one of his whist partners, with whom he played in the Grape Restaurant nearly every day after his court rose, was a priest.

On family walks, Grandpa, a tall, thin, handsome man with wiry grey hair, marched with a firm, long step, well ahead of us. My small, round grandmother and I lagged behind. Sometimes he stopped, a flower in his hand, and explained to me how to recognise a genuine camomile plant, or in which soil speedwell or globe-flowers grew. In summer, he wore white linen trousers, a striped jacket and a peaked cap. Everyone far and wide knew Mr Sieger, the judge, and elderly people could remember him with affection even fifty years later.

The heavenly memories of my childhood also include Mr Beran, the tramp. Beran was a fairy-tale grandfather with a bushy mane of white hair, a white beard and forget-me-not blue eyes below thick eyebrows. He appeared each year when the cold wind began to blow on the stubble fields, in October or November.

'Your worship, it's cold outside and I can't keep warm in the haystack, lock me up,' he would ask, and under some fictitious conviction the judge would provide him with government shelter in the courthouse lock-up. I often went there. If Beran was not there, the lock-up was mostly empty and only a white flag fluttered on the courthouse. The lock-up was quite a pleasant and warm room, with an oak table, bench and bunk. The food for prisoners was the same as for the warden and was cooked by the warden's wife.

Beran was never much of an expense to the state because during the winter months he went around cleaning rugs for the more prosperous families, and he split wood and earned some money before moving on. My friends and I probably liked him the best of the adults. As soon as I came home from school, I threw my bag in a corner and sought out Beran. At noon, he sat on a stool in a corner of our large kitchen, eating his meal with the plate on his knees. He always knew how to please the cook. He told each and every one of them, 'Your cooking is the best in Mnichovo Hradiště!' When we had both finished our meal, the girls from the neighbourhood came and we sat around kind old Beran and he told us stories from his life as a tramp. What was true and how much he made up wasn't significant – he had God's gift as a storyteller and we sat spellbound.

The Jizera river, wild, yet with quiet nooks, has been my family's river for generations, the river of their youth. When my mother, Anči, was little, Františka used to take her to the ladies' river pool to teach her to swim. Grandfather Bondy took Anči's older brother, Vilík, to the gentlemen's pool. Between the cabins-on-stilts and some steps was a strip of about 300 metres of common land where, in swimsuits which covered rather than revealed, the ladies and gentlemen met. The years before World War I were relatively happy, and the family enjoyed these pleasant interludes. Much later, from my point of view, the river was an all-important place, because who knows whether it was there that 'my grandpa' began to hover around my already married grandmother?

The Jizera was also the river of my own childhood and even those cabins were still there. My grandfather Sieger taught me to swim in the river's chilly water with its strong current. I was not allowed to go there alone, or with girl friends, but more than once I sneaked away and broke that rule. Sometimes, sitting by the river on the steps of the ladies' cabins, I daydreamed well beyond a reasonable hour and got home at dusk. My kind, loving grandfather was so worried about me that once he severely smacked me for this.

My childhood years before World War II were happy ones. I had two homes, both full of love and comfort: one with my parents in Josefov on the Metuje river and one with my grandparents in Mnichovo Hradiště. From my third year until the German occupation in 1939, I lived with my grandparents. When I was older and asked my mother why this was, I never received a satisfactory answer. But there was nothing to complain about. My childhood was happy and is part of my heavenly memories.

I grew quickly, and in height caught up with my grandmother. But in other ways? Even now I do not know. She was a fine woman – clever, well-educated, kind, tolerant and understanding. She never wasted words and whatever she said was impressive. She had matriculated from the Royal Austrian Girls' College, which was a rare achievement in those days. But Czech, rather than German, was her mother tongue. She spoke it formally, but with no affectation or snobbery. Otherwise she could not have coped with her second husband, who was an ardent lover of the Czech language. Grandfather read widely, detective stories as well as scholarly works, and reading with a pencil in his hand he would underline any grammatical errors and send the offending book back to the publishers.

Grandmother was an outstanding pianist and gave some concerts. Her admiration for Wagner and Grandfather's passionate advocacy of the Czechs Dvořák and Smetana often resulted in forceful and very loud arguments. The conflict usually began when they were choosing music: what will we play today? They often played duets, so they argued frequently. The arguments were really quite amicable, they evoked neither fearfulness nor anxiety in me and normally ended agreeably. The issue was not only about what was to be played, but also *how.* They had very different temperaments. Grandmother's playing was precise and sometimes this annoyed Grandfather. She never missed a beat, unlike Grandpa who was a genius at improvising and could play in his own style, even the most difficult pieces. Grandma played exclusively from the music and Grandpa grunted that she was 'just a woman' and was therefore lacking in rhythm. Incidentally, that is how I also turned out. I too had no rhythm.

The piano was not only a source of pleasure but of misery too. Quite often I arrived late for afternoon school because Grandpa would not allow me to leave home until I had played a small piece exactly to his liking. Then, after the bell had rung, I crawled along the corridor so that the caretaker wouldn't catch me. I was not particularly afraid. I knew that if the headmistress, Mrs Šorejsová (who had taught my mother), caught me and I told her the truth, she would not risk scolding Grandpa. Sometimes I misused this alibi and, even after the bell had rung, calmly slid on the ice down the hill on my schoolbag.

In 1938 I finished primary school in Mnichovo Hradiště and, by the skin of my teeth, completed an entrance exam for the first year of college in Mladá Boleslav. I was terribly proud that each day I would travel to school by train with the older college students. My pride was short-lived. During mobilisation the trains did not run for several weeks and my family decided that I would attend the state school in the town square near the courthouse. I think they also made this decision because they feared for my safety – daily travel did not appeal to them now. I didn't even stay at the state school for more than a year. Our class teacher, Mr Rejzek, wept as he sat behind his desk on 15 March 1939, the day the Germans invaded our country. We girls wept with him. We draped a mourning veil over our picture of Tomáš Masaryk, the first President of Czechoslovakia, who had not lived to witness this tragic day.

In September 1937 Grandfather Sieger had written one of his poems in my autograph book.

My dearest child
In life you cannot only weep,
In life you must also smile.
With life itself you need to fight
Always with truth, never with lies.

Perhaps it seems like an old man's story
And I must not interfere
With the path of youth
Into the adult world of experience.

Always try to learn more,
Smile at work and in life,
Always try, and, with a little luck,
Life will be more readily endured.

Never expect more than life can give –
Live it joyfully
But never play games with it.

Who would not like to 'play with life' at ten years old? But it happened that life played with me and not in a fair way. The German occupation interfered with everything, even with the mundane things of everyday life. Most of all, I learnt something important which, until then, had been unknown to me – that I was Jewish, that Grandmother was Jewish, Mother and Father too, and all our relatives on both sides of the family. It was a pretty long line of people, all respected citizens: my dear uncles, aunts and cousins. The Nuremberg Laws instantly made them second-class citizens.

In 1940 I had to return to my parents' home in Josefov, a fortress town built in the time of Emperor Josef II, a town which was strange and mysterious and which, until then, had represented the most blissful part of the year for me: holidays. I must admit that, with my restless soul, my return to Josefov would have been a welcome change, if it had not been for an edict forbidding travel on public transport. This cut us off from my grandparents and them from us.

As our contact with the world diminished, my maturity and my experience of a previously unknown emotional world were accelerated. Only then did I reach for a little brown book with gold trimming and my initials J.R.F. on it. It was a diary which my father had given me for Christmas 1938. Later it would be hidden in our house by a friend until my return at the end of World War II.

My first conversation with my diary is dated 18 September 1940.

I received this diary a while ago, but for a long time I couldn't get down to writing in it. Now, writing in it has given me a friend with whom I can talk as much as I want and who will not betray me. My dear friend diary, you could have a happy friend if ... if only times were not as difficult as they are now. I am thirteen years old. The blow which changed everything was struck on 15 March 1939. On that day, the Germans occupied our country and, as time passes, things are getting worse and worse. I am 'un-Aryan', therefore I cannot go to school or to the cinema. A German commissioner [Treuhändler] has been installed in Father's business. My parents are constantly annoyed about it (I am not surprised) and, often, I suffer from their anger. Now I am taught at home from school texts by our acquaintance Mr Winternitz, with whom I always argue. He has prepared a daily timetable of study for me, so that I don't become lazy and stupid.

Often I feel like crying. Perhaps my greatest unhappiness is Mother

8

or Father telling me that I am not good, that I only annoy them and don't give them any joy. I try to be as good as I can, but sometimes I can't help being naughty. Surely all children are naughty sometimes, and I am still a child. I am only thirteen. According to my timetable, I have piano practice from 2 to 3 p.m., and from 3 to 5 p.m. revision of 'school' work for Mr Winternitz. That means I have no free time. Probably no other child in Josefov has such a burden!

When the weather is beautiful I slave away and as soon as the sun sets I am allowed outside. I don't go out. Why would I? All the girls are outside earlier than I and, later on, I have no one to speak to, walk with, or to help roast potatoes on an open fire. If I break these rules, I get smacked.

After just such an incident, I felt the need to begin writing this diary. After writing the first few lines, I had to go and chop up mushrooms. It wasn't until after dinner that I could write any more. Now I have to sleep and here ends this memorable day.

I like writing a diary very much and tomorrow, if possible, I'll continue.

At that time I was a chubby child, a wide-eyed girl with curly brown hair. Despite the racial restrictions, boys admired me. This annoyed father, who regarded me as a child, and strictness was his idea of how to bring up a daughter, occupation or no occupation. 'You have to be better than everyone else and know more,' was one of his favourite sayings. I realise, today, that he was right but, then, it bothered me. I had to do more than I would have liked to, yet I could do almost nothing. I derived my fun by going against everything and everyone, by committing various misdemeanours against the Germans and against my parents.

I lived my own secret life. In the study, books covered one whole wall and, instead of learning algebra, I read *Madame Bovary*. The window facing the street was my world. The fortress of Josefov, this town of barracks, had a simple layout. The town's streets crisscrossed, in a similar way to those I would later see in Terezín and, to the left, I could see as far as the fountain in the square. The only house on the right prevented my imagining a road to infinity – no villages, no little towns, a road leading nowhere. I more or less knew the three thousand residents of our town by sight. The rest were only green German uniforms.

On the left, I could not only see the fountain but also the footpaths around the square where everyone promenaded on Sundays. It was not so long ago that I too had giggled with the other girls, and the boys had teased us, pulled our hair and secretly slipped us little notes. I went there one day, the yellow star on my woollen coat and, would you believe – success! I held a squashed-up note in my pocket and flew home. What has he written to me, this very mature seventeen-year-old idol of Josefov girls' hearts? He really flattered me, this handsome fellow with curly black hair and an impossible Christian name and surname – Adolf Hroch: hroch in Czech means hippopotamus. But after my 'literary' education from the European Literature Club, and with my precocious thirteen-year-old's notions, I was contemptuous of his declaration of love à la Mills and Boon, which I secretly read. He wrote how charming my big black eyes were, etc. Forever yours, Adolf. All right, I could stand the name Hroch, but *Adolf*? Nevertheless, at the cinema on the following Sunday, I stood with the others and for one crown watched the film *Eve Is Being Silly,* and didn't remove my hand when he grabbed it in the dark.

The ban on visiting public places, including cinemas, ultimately could not be ignored. The promenade was not part of any ordinance but, day by day, it became harder to ignore the fear shown by others. In Josefov there were only three Jewish families, including ours, and only one Jewish thirteen-year-old girl – me.

So what was left? The capacity to fall desperately in love, even platonically, and this I did. Every day, the German soldiers strode to the drill-square past the window through which I gazed left and right. They marched and sang 'Lili Marlene' or some other hackneyed tune. It was just like the films. It's strange that it all seemed real. I ignored the green 'locusts', the German soldiers. I overlooked them but cannot say that I hated them – that feeling was unknown then – and a handsome prince rode his horse at their head. His cape fell onto the horse's flank. He held the reins lightly, he looked far ahead, beyond the horizon, to infinity.

I daydreamed. My prince and I, he with a scar across his gentle, pale cheek, were the main players. For weeks and weeks I waited for the moment when he would ride past my window and would turn and free me, because he had been waiting only for me and, at first sight, had fallen in love. My prince's name was 'Poem'. Platonic love for a young German officer was filled with guilt. 'I dare not, I cannot, because ...' I comforted myself with the thought that he did not wish to be an officer in the armed forces, the *Wehrmacht*, but his family had insisted, and he was so young ...

29 September 1940. *I had no time to write anything yesterday, but on the whole nothing much happened. In the morning, my parents went to Hradec Králové to meet Grandpa. I am not permitted to be in Mnichovo Hradiště now, but it doesn't bother me much. Here in Josefov I have Mother and Father and I can run around outside more. So, my parents left and I had a French lesson with Miss Ryllová. She's a really nervy lady and if you make a mistake she hits the roof.*

Miss Ryllová is tall and skinny and she wears long, narrow skirts and lace blouses with high, starched collars. She looks like a character from a romantic novel. It is said that she was very beautiful when she was young and two officers fought a duel over her. Duelling was not unusual here as there were many officers in the barracks. Even among our acquaintances there was a general, but the Germans arrested him. The young man whom Miss Ryllová loved was shot in the duel. He's buried in the cemetery on the hill behind the fortress. There are hundreds of graves there, of soldiers killed in the 1866 war between Austria and Prussia. The battle was nearby and they say that 'a river of blood flowed from it.' My French teacher never married and she remained faithful to her officer. Perhaps that's why she's so edgy. Mother also has French conversation lessons with her. It's sometimes unbearable with Miss Ryllová, usually because I am not well-prepared and read from the textbook upside down, which I know how to do quite well.

In the afternoon my parents and Grandpa returned and I was very glad. I love my grandparents so much. There was a continual stream of visitors, so for a while I went off to the Sokol [Sports Organisation] *Stadium which is just behind our house. If the weather is fine, there is always someone about. Boys and girls train for athletics and play volleyball. In winter we ice-skate there. But probably next winter I won't be able to because the new ordinances now forbid my going to Sokol. I couldn't stay long so I went home.*

12 October 1940. *I should have confessed my silly infatuation with Poem (unfortunately German) to the priest, this being the biggest sin of my life, but I was cured by a new deep feeling. But this time it's probably real love. I'm a bit scared to write about it. What if someone*

11

found my diary? But I'd better write something. Mr Winternitz was not very successful at educating me and so my parents found a new tutor for me, a paid one. He is a student at the Jaroměř College (there isn't one in Josefov). It was, and is, terribly risky to tutor in a Jewish family in 1940. I think he accepted because he needed money for his mother and brother. Mr Miroslav is illegitimate, his mother is an alcoholic and his brother is backward. They live together in a council shelter where they pay no rent. When his mother is slightly sober she earns some money from cleaning, but Miroslav is the main breadwinner. He was accepted into college because his entrance exams were better than all the other students' and, from his first year, he gave private lessons. Incidentally, he also went to the entrance exam secretly and of his own accord.

I assume that my parents pay him enough for him to risk coming here. If a prototype could exist for the Aryan race, Miroslav would qualify perfectly: 185 centimetres tall, slim, with straight blond hair, a narrow Nordic head, blue eyes and a straight nose. Every physical attribute is beautiful. He looks like Gary Cooper. Only his lips are a little bit narrow. He hardly ever smiles. Actually, he has no reason to. His life was, and is, remarkably difficult. Of course, for quite a while I have known him by sight. In our small town with its curious combination of soldiers and civilians, he couldn't go unnoticed. He was always alone, always lost in thought and contemptuous of others. Often, while I gazed out of the window, I saw his stick-like figure. He always dresses meticulously and conservatively. He is regarded as being the best student in the Jaroměř College since its foundation more than fifty years ago. Even by the Metuje riverside he lies alone on a rug and reads. Studies? I don't know.

Then he appeared at our house. He is polite and aloof. He is supposed to teach me second- and third-year subjects, including Latin. I spend two hours a day with him and for the rest of the day I study alone. It's a pain. Perhaps I learn something, sometimes, but I am absolutely unable to 'perform' for him. Whenever the doorbell rings around the time he comes, I shake like a leaf. It is love, deep and agonisingly hopeless. I am thirteen and he is eighteen. Even if I were not Jewish I wouldn't have a chance. It is completely different from my Poem. Mr Miroslav sits next to me when he checks my homework and I feel the touch of his sleeve, I hear his breath. To my horror, I also hear his angry condemnations and sharp words when my maths solutions are wrong. And that is often. My mathematics is hopeless and I mix up Latin vocabulary when I am flustered. In brief, I am a terrible student.

16 October 1940. *While walking with a girl friend, we met* him. *Can you believe it, diary, he greeted me. If I'm about to meet* him, *I start shaking and make a detour around the whole town. I don't know what's the matter with me. He is surly, almost nasty. I know that it's the way it is and, sometimes, I am glad to have him like this. Anyway, I am just a little girl and I wouldn't like to go around with him. I know that other girls go to the park with boys, even older ones, and they kiss each other. But me, never. So it's just as well that Mr Miroslav is only my dream and my best friend Jarka is the only one who knows about him.*

5 November 1940. *I still think about him first thing when I wake up in the morning, and when I go to sleep he is in my mind. Now, I am determined to know everything perfectly because it is terrible when he looks so unkind when I answer incorrectly or, if I am ruffled, not at all. It doesn't surprise me. I would be just as annoyed if I were in his shoes. But he doesn't know why I am so brainless. I really do know much more than I am able to tell him. This morning, during the time permitted for Jews to be outside, I went to buy a pad of drawing paper and saw him walking in the square with other boys and girls. I was overwhelmed with anger. Why is he not alone? Why am I just his student? For him I am simply a little girl and he looks down at me from the top of his willowy frame. The condescending lout. And because I am afraid that he won't even greet me, I avoid the square and sometimes even whole blocks of houses and the barracks.*

I honestly don't like walking past the barracks because the soldiers who hang out of the windows do not know that I wear a yellow star and they call after me in the same way as they do to other girls. It's impossible to describe how silly I am. I criticise other girls when they allow boys to make fun of them and lead them up the garden path, but what about me? I'm a hundred times more stupid.

20 November 1940. *I must tell you, dear diary, that I am very happy being at home. I only regret that Grandma and Grandpa have been abandoned. Grandfather, our Aryan in the family, can occasionally come when he decides to leave Grandmother alone. He is coming next*

Monday and I am looking forward already to his visit. From time to time, Father lectures me fiercely: how I must study, why I must know more than other girls from Josefov, and so on. Apparently I must counterbalance how badly others treat us with my superior knowledge. Usually it occurs precisely when I am studying and he holds me up. If I ever have children I will remember how I was at thirteen. Papa never does. He says that no one told him to study because when he was thirteen he had no parents: his mother died when he was nine, his father when he was eleven. There were seven siblings and they looked after each other. They all completed their education, at least at college. Ha! All of them! His youngest brother shot himself when he was nineteen, possibly because of an unhappy love affair. He was supposedly as pretty as an angel. Perhaps I take after his tendency towards unrequited love? So it's always 'learn! learn!' I definitely have plenty of good intentions, but then I watch the clouds and the hours fly by. What can I do?

The increasing severity of Nazi ordinances has solved my problem. One day, my tutor came and said that he hadn't time to come to us any more. Why, why did he think up such a silly excuse? We understood, but now I have no lessons. That really hurts me. My Mr Miroslav, tall, thin and handsome, also said that he was warned by a colleague not to come to our house. I was so disappointed. I can say that he was my first love, even if he didn't know it. Probably I'll never stop loving him. I am trying to forget him, but it's impossible. I am now going to the dentist in Jaroměř with Mother, and I hope I'll bump into him. Since he stopped coming to our home, I have seen him about three times. I know that it's pointless, I should be worrying about other things. There are so many tragic events, that even to myself I appear completely ridiculous.

Of their own accord, my parents told their remaining non-Jewish friends not to visit us. Our house, the biggest Jewish house in Josefov and Jaroměř, gradually became a dormitory. 'All' the local Jews were moved to our place. Father's former business office and shop were also used as living space. Nobody asked how we would all fit in. Mr Laufer died just in time. Pepík Winternitz, an old bachelor, was a family friend and it was a good thing that he lived with us. An old couple who were very sweet, the Steins, lived in our study and I liked going there for Granny-like hugs. And then there was a couple with two grown-up sons who all looked the way people believed Jews were supposed to look: rather small, round, big-nosed, with protruding eyes behind glasses. I couldn't stand the two young men, Fricek and Oswald. They took liberties with me. I told Father that Fricek once touched my breast and remarked that I had big 'tits' and I didn't know what he meant. Without a word, Father gave him such a punch that he fell to the ground. From that time a silent animosity grew between our families. They stopped playing chess with my father and we all ignored each other.

The most interesting new arrivals for me were a young family, originally from Carpathian Ruthenia (part of Czechoslovakia before World War II), who had come to our region. A husband, wife and two small children. They were arrested after a few weeks and imprisoned in Hradec Králové, supposedly for stealing. Four-year-old Betulinka and one-year-old Jiříček were left behind in our house. I took them under my wing and was mother to them. I had ceased studying anyway because it was impossible in that madhouse. They were beautiful, delightful and timidly quiet children. It was as if their fate were written on their pale faces and in their large, black eyes. I loved them. I slept next to them. I changed Jiříček's nappies and I fed him. At the age of fourteen I took over the mothering of two children who would later be taken from me.

15 January 1941. Shame, shame, shame, diary I must sincerely apologise. I haven't written for so long I don't know where to start.

First of all, my friendship with Jarka Torská. We used to be inseparable friends but now she doesn't want to visit me even though we still like each other. It's up to me to contact her. When I do, everything is so pleasant and we get on so well. In sunny weather, we used to go for a walk nearly every day. Around Josefov there are three walks – mostly alleys of chestnut and tall lime-trees. We used to collect chestnuts and carve mushrooms and other things out of them. In autumn, the paths are covered with layers of leaves, and even though I am getting older I always make long leaf chains which I pull behind me like a bridal train, imagining what that would be like. In spring, Josefov is clothed in green, and in winter you can toboggan down the slopes. Best of all we like the path facing north towards the Krkonoše mountains. We know almost every tree there. I don't know why, but we both love this walk. Late in autumn, when the cold winds began to blow, we had to give up our walks but then we looked forward to snow and skiing.

Jarka was the daughter of a Ukrainian refugee, Michael Torský, who fled from the Russian Revolution. Mr Torský was employed in our business. He joined the Germans and forbade Jarka to visit us. For a while we met secretly, but later Jarka thought that I didn't like her because I was always correcting her and she couldn't stand it. I mourned her loss. But this was not the worst thing. I learnt to be alone, to go on long walks in the alleys behind the ramparts of our town, to dream and to turn inwards, even from my parents. I created my own world into which nobody was allowed. I became conscious of the new ordinance: 'People who have contact with Jews will lose their clothing coupons, their children will be forbidden to attend school and they will be required to wear the star!'

10 February 1941. Now, as I have no friends, I walk by myself or with my mother. And perhaps it is better this way. When I gaze upwards, even the sky needs a lot of thinking about. I am always amazed by the beautiful vista of the Orlický and Krkonoše mountains. But sometimes I wish there was someone with whom I could express my feelings and share all this beauty. It is difficult to absorb it on my own. That's why I have you, diary, and now you are my best friend who reveals nothing!

Usually, I have to steal moments to write in my diary. From early morning I have plenty to do: I sweep out the kitchen stove (which doesn't really need much coal), light it, and prepare breakfast. The day revolves around housework, school books and time at the piano. It's about nine in the evening, my bedtime, before I find time for you, my diary.

20 September 1941. I am glad that Milka, the housemaid, has had to leave.

This is how it happened. For years and years Mařenka Žofáková served us as our cook, maid and nanny, all in one. She seemed like a member of the family. From my earliest years she crooned me to sleep, sang hymns and read fairy tales. She had a high, slightly screechy soprano voice. She was a strongly committed Catholic and so her songs were full of holy events and good deeds. I loved her. She was very kind and sometimes I took advantage of that. I can't remember the exact date, perhaps it was 1939 or 1940, when Mařenka broke her arm very badly.

She had no close family, but had inherited the right to occupy one room in a relative's cottage in a nearby village. So she left, and my parents temporarily took in Milka.

Milka had thick, straight, rusty-gold hair, sharp piercing green eyes, a pointy nose and thin lips, and a small figure which widened from the waist down. She was very determined and energetic. At a time when events had made us feel threatened on all sides, we had someone in the apartment whom we didn't know, and who was short-tempered, touchy and aggressive. Mother and Father told me discreetly that they were afraid of her and would try to get her off their hands. But it wasn't simple, as she would have to leave of her own accord. She did not want to leave, probably she liked it there. Mother lent her dresses for balls and she had time off whenever she liked. We were all glad when she wasn't at home. Because of Milka, our behaviour was artificial. And then she began to threaten us (not face to face but quite audibly) that if she didn't get this or that, including Mother's dresses and stockings, she would denounce us and we would have to 'go'.

The new regulation that Jews could not have servants under forty years of age disposed of Milka for us. I was grateful to the Germans for that. We ourselves could not get rid of Milka because of the possibility of her taking revenge on us. She was made to leave without our interference. For a while, my parents were afraid that she might have known too much about us. One of the dangers was to have more food than was in the rations, and it was impossible to hide this from Milka. People in the surrounding villages, who had always liked Father, supplied us really well.

20 September 1941. Since Milka (who was not from Josefov) disappeared for good, we are better off. Now we have a woman who comes to help twice weekly and, otherwise, I clean and help in the kitchen. I am cautious about writing down her name. I go with her and cut grass for our rabbits as we have no meat rations. Everything at home runs smoothly without Milka. I have lots of work but I don't mind.

25 November 1941. My friends have deserted me, one after the other. My friendship with Tamara and Kvĕta didn't appear to be as strong as with Jarka Torská but, even so, Jarka has gone too. I am not really sorry – the friendship began, then evaporated. Probably I didn't like her as much as I thought I did.

27 November 1941. For a long time, I have been putting off writing about one terrible thing that has happened to our family. Maybe it is because I have such strange feelings about it. The Gestapo are holding Father in Hradec Králové. I should be terribly miserable, but I'm not as miserable as I ought to be. I don't know why. Am I so hard or insensitive? I don't know. I am puzzled and can only explain that there is so much pain, despair and sorrow around us that I have no right to be indulgent. Perhaps it's because the Germans said that in one month everything would be sorted out. It's an endlessly long month and I reproach myself for not thinking more about Father. I would miss Mother much more. Without her, even hours would seem endless. Sometimes, I am almost glad that Father is not here, but I can only confess this to you, dear diary. He was so unhappy, so nervous at losing his business, that I often felt angry with him, and shouldn't have. I don't know what sort of a person I am. My thoughts are quite unsuitable. Probably I am unable to write clearly what I feel. Sometimes I am madly happy, and sometimes I am engulfed by fits of sadness. To cover up the sadness, I frown. Then Father grumbles at me – that I am awful, have such an unpleasant expression and increase his bad moods and worries. It's too much for me and I begin to cry. When he asked why I was crying, I couldn't and wouldn't answer him. So, 'even though you are almost an adult, you are an awful, whingeing girl' (according to Father).

I am not writing very positively about my father, even though I love him very much and I know what a fine person he is. Well, I am what I am, and I don't know what I am. I don't know what I think and what I should think in order to be good. I ponder and ponder, and in the end I have an empty, dull mind. I am miserable that I have no idea what I want. I am not studying at all. I help, I clean, I sweep out the rabbits' cage and clean up after the goose. I am happy doing this and quite satisfied. I am overjoyed that we no longer have a girl here, one feels quite differently. The household used to be upset by that stranger.

There is still so much to tell, but the washing-up must be done. Bye-bye, my diary, good night.

30 January 1942. A lot of snow has fallen this winter and with the snow came Christmas. The 'kind' Germans thought of more edicts for us: a ban on travelling beyond the district's boundary. So they cut us off from Grandfather and Grandmother. I couldn't imagine how they would live through Christmas without us. Christmas in our family used to be the most beautiful time of the year. Grandpa would set up a huge wooden nativity scene on a chest next to the piano in the sitting room. The whole city of Bethlehem was created on three levels and was placed on green paper sprinkled with pebbles. There were sheep, shepherds and kings, and one king stood with splendid camels. The star of Bethlehem shone over everything. In the middle of the room there was a tree which always reached the ceiling, while beneath it were lots of presents. It was almost impossible to wait for the special evening meal to finish, before opening the dining-room door to that mysterious room which was firmly locked for four days before Christmas Eve. We were always, always together. And now? I cried in sorrow and anger. Then it dawned on me that I could visit them secretly. I would go without the 'star' and I wouldn't be noticed. I told my parents and they, the loves, agreed. I stayed home on Christmas Eve so that they wouldn't be sad, and I left two days later. Everything was very discreet, we didn't even let my grandparents know. Nobody could have imagined the shock, surprise and joy in the expressions on their faces. How glad I was that I had come.

31 January 1942. *As I had to go to sleep, my real description of the visit to Mnichovo Hradiště had to wait until today.*

It was almost dark when I arrived in Hradiště. Everyone knew me, but I was fortunate enough to slip through the town without any 'good citizen' seeing me and possibly reporting me to the police. It was snowing lightly. The festive evening had emptied the streets and I felt as if I were in a strange dream. The snow muffled my footsteps and I had the feeling that I was on a secret mission. I arrived at our house and, unnoticed, climbed to the first floor. I was lucky – the doors to the apartment hallway were partly open. I sidled through them, and from the dark passage went into the well-lit, pleasantly warm living-room which I like so much. In that moment, they both saw me. Initially their faces showed shock and surprise but then radiated joy. It was the best Christmas present they could give me. I was perfectly happy. I spent the days with Grandma, until she told me that I was with Grandpa and herself too much, and should visit friends of my own age, or invite them to us. We all hoped that the terrible edicts against the Jews wouldn't affect Grandmother because Grandfather's 'Aryanness' would protect her. Grandfather even tried to adopt me as his own child, but that didn't help.

I can still recall how beautiful that Christmas was. The girls in Hradiště were not afraid to invite me out, and so I experienced my first party, with gramophone music, dancing, and boys. Everyone was older than I, and because it was the first time I had been with sixteen- to eighteen-year-old boys and girls, I felt rather awkward. First of all we played rummy, then we rolled up the rug, blacked out the windows and danced. I felt a little uncomfortable and did not speak the whole afternoon, but when Pepík Cerman invited me to dance I forced myself to join him. Then he started to flirt with me and sang a sentimental song in my ear, 'Hm, hm, oh you are beautiful', and another one, 'When I see some girls' dark brown eyes, I can't go to sleep ...' Then he walked me home and put his arm around my shoulder and gave me a kiss. But I moved, so it was on my cheek. I am writing so much about this because, so far, it was my greatest adventure. I also had a guilty conscience because in these sad times I was having fun. I was glad to be in my warm room again, shielded by my grandparents from feelings for which I wasn't ready.

Later on, another really important event occurred. Mother's brother Vilík, whom I adore, arrived from Prague. He isn't married. He is very handsome and from the time I was very young I used to go skiing on the Krkonoše mountains with him. Although he was hard on me sometimes – I had to ski as many kilometres as the adults despite being very tired – I loved these trips. It's impossible now because we are not allowed. No car, no trips. He too came secretly, and it was wonderful.

I was in Hradiště more than a month. And then came the time to leave! Grandpa and Grandma tried not to cry in front of me, but Grandma failed and Grandpa had tears in his eyes. I was leaving them and I was sadder than I had ever been in my life. Grandpa can go out to play cards with his friends and he can even visit us in Josefov, but Grandmother ... it's futile to comment. She is ashamed to go out in public, so she hardly ever leaves the house.

The train journey went without a hitch. I was so warmly welcomed at home that I wouldn't change places with a princess. The daily routine has been established once more.

Violet

More than fifty years have passed since twenty-year-old Jarmila Holatová's life ended. All that time, I have felt indebted to her. Shortly after the end of the most terrible war in the history of mankind, a war which managed to snare more victims than any other, I knew that there was only one way for me to repay this debt – to tell Jarmila Holatová's story. No headstone exists where flowers can be laid on her grave, nor will the dates of her birth and death appear in history books.

I have been delaying the moment when I would sit in front of a blank sheet of paper and write the first sentence. Why? I really do not know the exact answer. Because the events of those years affected me too deeply? Because the gift of life my parents and I received from this girl was too great? The effort involved in this undertaking, and the effort to awaken the reader's desire to read to the end is taxing. But there is no other way.

My dear Jarmilka, again and again I have read your few letters which were all that remained of you, and which were hidden in the lining of my coat and journeyed with me not only *to* the concentration camp but, by a twist of fate, *from* it. Our friendship was short, not quite two years. Those years were grim: 1941 and 1942. We were not destined to share a lifelong friendship. Your elegant handwriting revealed many unusual characteristics – you were of above-average intelligence and, for your age, extremely mature. Above all, you were warm-hearted, kind and unselfish.

I have waited a long time, so that through recounting your fate I could express the absurdity of that war. You and I have been drawn into 'history'. Even after so many years, I don't know whether I have attained the necessary detachment to be able to write about what happened. There is no detachment from pain, no absence of pain, even now. It is said that pain fades away. Really? I think not, not all. It is not possible to forget everything and everyone. And one should not. Your death and the deaths of millions like you should never be forgotten, nor should the pain be repressed.

The passenger train laboriously chugged from Jaroměř-Josefov towards Mnichovo Hradiště. In early 1941, Bohemia was experiencing a piercingly cold winter. It was minus 15° centigrade outside and only a little less cold in the unheated carriages. Mother and I perched restlessly on the hard wooden benches, our coats wrapped around our bodies so that as little heat as possible would escape. Outside the dirty carriage window, it was snowing and snowing, thickly and frighteningly. I have always loved snow but those pieces of falling ice did not resemble the tenderness of fluffy snowflakes which settle on one's eyelids and lips, and melt so quietly. Did the war change even snowflakes? Not so long ago, the same train journey had been an adventurous expedition to the unknown – my head out of the window, the wind ruffling my hair, the glowing sparks disappearing to who knows where? The war also changed that. Now we just wished that the journey would finish as quickly as possible. It was our last trip, taking us to our dearest relations, Grandma and Grandpa. Already it was risky, because yet another ordinance of 1941 against Jews was imminent: they would be forbidden to travel on public transport and prohibited from crossing from one district to another. Each week, similar ordinances appeared. The one that separated us from our dear family before death did was the most cruel.

The train splutters and stops with a jolt. Železný Brod. A few 'snowmen' get on, shaking their coats, fur caps and jackets, the snow turning into dirty puddles on the floor. One figure, a more slender snowman, shakes off the snow. Blue eyes shine brightly above a large chenille scarf and below it hangs a thin grey coat, far too thin for the cold weather, and in it a girl. For me, a near-fourteen-year-old, she is a young lady. But this young lady looks exactly as Snow White could and must have! I couldn't take my eyes off her – her long, wavy light-brown hair, her straight delicate nose, high forehead, determined chin, unusually luminous eyes. A deep, melodic voice speaks. The young lady asks politely if she may sit down. Mother moves across, and in my mind I shout yes, please sit with us, from the first glimpse I like you. But my eyes are staring at the dirty floor and do not want to budge. I am embarrassed in front of this young lady, in whose eyes I must be only a small, uninteresting girl.

In the murky winter daylight, the train begins to move reluctantly. But not for long. With a hollow, strange noise, it stops. The lights go out.

On the right, hidden by snow, is the Jizera river. On the left are rocks from which a waterfall of slivered ice hangs. In the middle of the track there is some unknown obstacle. This setting creates an impression that we are in no-man's land. It is not an unpleasant feeling. In these times, surely it would be easiest to plummet and disappear? So the news, that an avalanche has fallen on the track and no one knows how long it will take to clear, only extends this dream state. We wait.

I do not know how long we sat in the deepening twilight. It did not seem that anyone was terribly worried. The occupation, with its oppressive worries which no one could ignore, an ever-present evil, turned our incident on the railway track into an insignificant, minor discomfort.

Inactivity was not my vivacious mother's style. Unexpectedly, she grabbed me by the hand and pulled me to the window in the corridor. She put her arms around my shoulders: 'I like the girl who sat down with us. Don't you?' Immediately, she answered herself. 'But of course, you must like her. And if you don't know how to meet her, I shall introduce you, all right?'

It was not really a question, Mother did whatever she wanted to. This time her decisiveness was in accordance with my wishes. It was exactly what I had wanted. My former girl friends were gradually fading away. Understandably. People had to care about the safety of their families. But write? Maybe she would, even Snow White. Maybe she would not be perturbed by the yellow star which marked me out from others when I walked through town. But shyness and fear of rejection led me to answer stubbornly, 'No, I don't want to, I don't care about anybody!'

'You silly goose,' said my mother. 'You really are impossible!' I knew she was right.

Little by little, the cold crept into every corner of the unlit carriage. The snow was blown through the partly opened window onto the opposite seat and formed a small pile. All of us put on whatever we could – awkward figures moving through the dark. Hands and feet felt frozen, and the carriage rocked rhythmically with the stamping of feet. Here and there laughter sounded.

'My' young lady suddenly sang: 'Underneath our tiny window appeared a mighty frost ...'

The masked figures joined in, sang and danced. I don't exactly know when I joined in the singing. Snow White's warm hand squeezed mine. Her palm spread warmth into mine, our fingers entwined. Then I hoped that the avalanche would never be cleared away. We could stay here and the warmth of our hands would spread all over. No Protectorate, no transports east into the unknown, no war. We would be covered in snow and the world would forget us.

But life does not fulfil wishes, particularly foolish ones.

The track was cleared and the train began to move slowly forward. A stream of glittering sparks shot out of the old locomotive's funnel, only to die quickly as they encountered snowflakes. Hazy light from the war-regulation tinted globes dimly illuminated our faces. I could see Snow White rummaging in her bag. She pulled out a piece of paper and a pencil.

She whispered, 'I am getting off, I'll write down my address. Write yours, please. I would like us to write.'

Suddenly, the gesture of friendship was made and it was unmistakable. For the first time I read the name Jarmila Holatová.

'But at home everyone always calls me Violet, apparently because of my eyes.' She smiled. 'It's ridiculous isn't it?'

But no, it wasn't ridiculous at all. It was lovely, and much more accurate than 'Jarmila'.

I had no time to hesitate. Disjointed sentences tumbled out – about my 'wrong', non-Aryan pedigree, of which I had known nothing until recently, a heritage that had made us lepers among innocents. The

24

reasons? I didn't know them. So how could I explain? I only knew that I wanted her to know the truth about the person to whom she was offering her friendship. Then she would have to decide for herself. Mother shook her head and furtively looked around for any listeners to my confession. We had unstitched the 'warning' stars from our coats, so that our journey would be easier. That was against the law. The yellow star with JUDE written on it in Gothic script had to be worn. If we were caught, a severe punishment would follow.

With a strange, breathless and almost wicked curiosity, I waited for Violet's reply. Just wait, I thought to myself, you will wince when you know ... and if you do want to write to a girl with a yellow star, your parents will forbid it. And ultimately they will be right, I conceded. In times like these, childhood vanishes in a matter of hours, not years.

Snow White listened quietly, intensely, and pretended that such a rigmarole was part of the daily chatter of her village. She did not even blink. At that moment the train braked to a halt and, without a reply, she tightly squeezed my hand and disappeared into the darkness of the tiny railway station. My heart ached. We had hardly had time to become friends and already I had lost her.

For the rest of the journey, Mother and I remained silent. For weeks I had been living for the meeting with my forsaken grandparents, but the weariness and sleepiness caused by many hours of increasing numbness robbed us of the sense of joyous expectancy. Without a word, Grandpa, our family's white Aryan sheep, squeezed me stiflingly in his arms. There was anxiety in that squeeze, as his long legs had measured the small platform for hours. My handsome, proud grandpa, who taught me everything that makes life joyful, cried. It was the first time I had ever seen him cry but, alas, not the last.

We began walking through the hushed town, blacked-out because of war. Not a soul anywhere. Mother and Grandpa spoke together and my head spun with memories – the first swimming strokes in the Jizera river that Grandpa taught me, the first carefree falls on skates and skis when I was five. He had taught me to read and enjoy books as a treat for finishing jobs, to recognise flowers and the stars in the sky, to bake potatoes in the ash of potato stalks, and to fly a kite on a really long string. He had taught me the endless longing for knowledge, and an almost inordinate belief in goodness, justice and love. And many other things too. Grandfather was a nonconformist. He himself followed no religious persuasion, and he squabbled with Grandmother who had been christened when Hitler was threatening Europe – not because of the christening, which had really been his idea, but because she was serious about some of the Christian beliefs and she encouraged me to be more than conciliatory.

Grandfather had left the Catholic Church as soon as he graduated from the Plzeň College. His objections were aimed at the Church itself. He believed in the revelations of nature, and in the ultimate strength of the human mind over matter. He was hot-headed, and any sort of doctrine was unacceptable to him. For us, there were to be no more discussions about the world. My own opinions were just forming and he would not live to see my adulthood. Time was not on our side. Grandpa would be executed in the Pankrác prison on 1 May 1944. But, luckily, at that moment I did not know what lay ahead.

From the station, we came to the main square with its complex of rectangular buildings in the middle: the Town Hall and Courthouse – Grandfather's domain. Until recently, my grandfather, dressed in judicial robes, and with a crucifix standing on his big oak desk, had meted out justice there. Along a short street there was the church. How many arguments we had had at home over that church! Grandpa's philosophical arguments were never victorious over the will of my tiny, clever and stubborn grandmother, so he used emotion.

'If you love this child,' he used to tell Grandma, 'don't let her kneel on those cold stones, she will catch a cold!'

But not even concern about my health influenced her. Grandmother had me as an ally. I loved the smell of May lilies and peonies in the church, and the sickly, bitter-sweet, almond smell of astras and autumn conifer needles. I was not prepared to give up the darkness and quietness of the church, nor the organ and the smell of incense during Mass. Grandpa lost this dispute with Grandma and me, and the Jewish side of the family embraced Catholicism. But with the Nuremberg Laws, we all lost: baptism certificates did not help, nor my genuinely trusting faith. To the German authorities I remained a Jew.

We reached my grandparents' house, the gate slamming behind us. I raced up the spiral staircase to the first floor like lightning. Up until that moment, I had not realised how desperately our arrival was awaited. My tiny grandmother (she only reached Grandpa's shoulder) had not come to meet us. Jews were forbidden to be in the streets after

9 p.m., but Grandma, with her unsuitable, un-Aryan blood, had expanded anti-Jewish edicts: she had decided not to leave the house until the end of the war. Calmly, but decisively, she refused to be told where she could or could not go, during which hours she was permitted to go shopping or be out of doors. She objected to reading the signs 'Jews Forbidden' on the gates into the Waldstein Chateau Park, where we used to stroll together, collecting chestnuts in the grove of trees and gathering flowers and vegetables from the gardener. She objected to chance meetings with acquaintances in the street, people who would be afraid to greet her, who would look aside, or would cross to the opposite footpath. She did not want to receive medical attention from a doctor whose waiting-room she would have to enter at a specified time, or to go on public transport in which, as a Jewess, she was required to stand on the rear platform. She resolved not to sew the yellow star onto her clothes. She willingly sentenced herself to virtual house arrest well before the Gestapo seized her. Such a resolution was not without consequences. Her sociable nature was encased in a shell. But the deep love of my grandfather was a great pillar of support. So also was Anna Heřmanová, their housekeeper.

For years, Anna had lived with our family, more friend than housekeeper and my 'Auntie'. Our Anna remained faithful to Grandfather and Grandmother until the last moment, even though she had to face attacks and threats from others. As a matter of fact, it was she who enabled my grandmother to achieve her self-imposed exile. She took charge of all contact with the outside world. She belonged among those good-hearted souls for whom a life of service really meant something.

I raced up the stairs, past the massive rail with its copper knobs which, long ago, had prevented my mother and Vilík from sliding down the banister. In a moment I arrived at the wide glass door and turned the door-handle. *The* door-handle. Later, in Terezín, I dreamt about this door-handle: a tiger's head, polished to a golden shine for festive days, with, under its nose, a protruding tongue with a marble on it. That marble prevented entry to our apartment. Those who did not know the secret of opening our door could not enter – you had to turn the handle while pressing the marble at the same time. It was a device that gave me a feeling of safety, and I divulged its secret to no one. After the war, I tried to find the door-handle but it had gone. Several families, strangers, had lived in the house. That night in 1941, I pushed the marble and went in. A tiny, slumped figure sat on the glory-box in the dim passage, immobile from long, anxious waiting. I knelt by her legs, buried my head in her lap and my grandmother sobbed quietly with relief. So did I.

It is four weeks later. Fire radiates behind the mica windows of the enormous American heater. The large, irregularly shaped room is softly lit by a Venetian glass chandelier. It is warm and lovely. The aroma from branches of fir mixes with the scent of baked apples. Windows covered by black wartime curtains, and a rug hanging over the balcony door, enhance the feeling of safety and homeliness. Grandpa sits in the old wing chair next to the heater, his long legs stretched out, and reads, while Grandma darns a sock and whispers with Mother. Sleep overcomes me.

What has changed? After all, everything is as it used to be. In the quietness of home, the tension of the long day's events changes into painful sleepiness. I struggle against falling asleep, just to savour every moment. For how long? Unedited images flicker beneath my eyelids. A train puffs and collapses into a snowdrift. Will-o'-the-wisp-like violet eyes entice me outside, into the snow. The train's door has a tiger-shaped handle, I turn and turn it, but cannot open it, and I wrestle futilely with the wind which pushes the door back. Grandmother is a small wooden figurine in my hands and cries out for us to stay ... Chaos. Dark lanes. I firmly hold onto Grandpa and we lose our way. The way home has been lost in the snow. We stagger against the wind, down snow-covered streets. I realise that we dare not sit down because we would freeze. But what a lovely sleep it would be ...

Grandmother kisses me on the forehead and says, 'Go to bed, my dear, you are terribly tired.'

I grab her around the neck. 'No, no, Grandma, I'm not.' It is then that I fall into a deep sleep.

I had remained in Mnichovo Hradiště alone. After three days, my mother had left to rejoin my father. She didn't want to leave him alone as it was only a few days since he had returned from the Hradec Králové gaol, where he had been imprisoned for six months by the Gestapo. He had been arrested because someone denounced him. Allegedly, he had concealed some goods during the transfer of his business to the German administrator, the *Treuhändler*. They found nothing. He returned from gaol undernourished, subdued and dispirited.

Regulations now stipulated that Jews must not be outside the boundary of their district (that given on their birth certificate) and after the four weeks I had to return to my parents. I left my beloved grandmother, who felt guilty that she had ruined my life because of her race. Yet for those four weeks I had lived behind doors in happy isolation from the world. We read, we played the piano, we even sang. Hidden behind Grandfather's beautiful bass-baritone voice, Grandmother, Mrs Anna and I sang carols, lullabies and some of my favourite songs such as 'Johnny grazed three oxen near the forest ...' Sometimes I couldn't sing the whole song because I sobbed about Johnny being bashed near the forest. And my grandfather's first name was John.

Mrs Anna looked after all the daily necessities. To the last, she remained discreet and humble, always on hand and understanding. The authorities, and certainly some other people, expected that she would be aware of her 'duty' and leave. She did not go.

The way home by train passed through Violet's countryside. In my mind I already called her nothing else. Thoughts about her were intense and sad. Sometimes I had a feeling that I knew her well, and knew what I could expect from her. At other times, I despairingly saw violet eyes like bottomless pools. Occasionally, in the night, I almost felt the warmth of her hand under the eiderdown. Often I daydreamed about her. While still in Mnichovo Hradiště, when the parquet floor creaked, with Grandmother reading late into the night and Grandfather sitting in his armchair clearing his throat, and while I lay in bed, she chatted to me.

Then I was home again. From the train, I rushed straight into Mother's arms. On the way home from the station, I automatically answered her questions, while I increased the pace of my steps until she could hardly keep up. Would a letter await me?

A pink envelope with gold edging and a neatly handwritten address, Miss Renée Friesová, Josefov on the Metuje River, was leaning against the inkstand on the small desk. My first impulse was to drop the suitcase and grab the envelope. No, I will not do that. I will unpack, have dinner with my parents ('Aren't you going to see who has written to you?' asked Mother, knowingly), wash the dishes, wash myself and, finally, at 9 o'clock, take this treasure to bed.

Apprehensively, I tore open the envelope and waited for the verdict. The letter was long. I devoured the words, the sentences, and read what, even in my most secret dreams, I could not have hoped for.

Violet clearly wishes that, in these trying times, we should become friends, and help each other live through the difficulties. Jarmilka's parents know of me and approve of our friendship. She offers to exchange her most secret thoughts, so that 'we shall get to know each other quickly and well.'

She describes her family. There are ten at home: mother, father, five brothers, herself and two sisters. For generations, the men in the family have been glassmakers. They blow and cut glass which resonates and is finely shaped. And because of that work, some members of the family die young from tuberculosis.

'We recently buried our brother Tony,' Violet wrote. 'As a matter of fact, there aren't ten of us, but nine. We live in a cottage built into the hillside near the forest. The narrow path through the snow to our house is now well trodden. We don't have much, but we can still afford to keep Minda the cat and Alík the dog.' Since the beginning of the occupation, Jarmilka and some other girls have been ordered to work in a textile factory in Tanvald. Because the country loco is usually late, they all often have to walk over the hill. It is very strenuous and she returns home very tired. But as soon as the door closes behind her, and the laughter of her smaller siblings shakes the cottage (it is a wonder it does not collapse), she is immediately refreshed.

With each letter, I learned more about the Holat family, who lived in the foothills of the Krkonoše mountains. The village of Jesenný was in the border region of the Sudeten Land. Violet was fearful for her father, who continued a family tradition of being a writer of local history. There were books on the shelf next to the stove in their little cottage, some which even belonged to her great-grandfather. When the whole family sat around the wooden, rectangular table in the evenings, her father would take a book, pull down the adjustable lamp and read. He did not have to read loudly, as they all listened attentively. Sometimes it was a tale from the Bible, other times from Czech legends.

'It is taken for granted in our family,' wrote Violet, 'that we older ones look after the small children, and I am almost a mother to them.'

For different reasons, we had both been drawn prematurely into the adult world. I had no brothers or sisters, but because of our situation under the occupation I matured quickly. I was brought up with ideals, but ideals which belonged to another time. 'If you are good, diligent and truthful, people will like you; everything you learn, from washing the dishes to Latin, is equally important in life.' All this belonged to the pre-war era, a carefree time, when I had been surrounded by love. Now I wore a warning star over my heart like a leper's bell, and this had quickly changed me. A sixteen-year-old girl, just over two years my senior, spoke adult words to me, and it was appropriate.

In one of my own early letters I tried to explain to Violet how my parents had agonised when they had to face the necessity of telling me that I was a Jew. Up until that time I honestly did not know. Even after March 1939, I conscientiously knelt by my bed before going to sleep, and said my favourite childhood prayer: 'Little angel, guardian mine, keep watch over my soul ...' and – as an encore, as well as a duty – 'Blessed be ...' realising that 'Little angel ...' was extremely childish for me.

Why did I embrace Catholicism? My father, whose parents were from the Těšín region on the Czech–Polish border, and had lived through a pogrom, was insistent that I should be christened as a baby. 'When she grows up, she can decide for herself,' Father had announced. He faced no maternal resistance. For generations, my mother's family had honestly tried to assimilate: they spoke Czech and had Czech sympathies. It became evident, however, that even the strongest attempt to escape from the medieval 'curse of the Jews' was completely unsuccessful. Much later, I heard the sentence: no matter how hard you try to forget your Jewish origin, someone will always remind you of it. I am glad that, despite my parents somehow thrusting this at me, I did not have to go through all that bother. Surprisingly, no one had ever screamed at me 'Jewess'. So I was not familiar with that term.

The occupation had now lasted for months, probably a year, and yet regularly on Sundays I wheedled silk stockings out of Mother to wear to Mass. The strict Maria Theresan church in Josefov's square had its own particular atmosphere. I ranked it among the pleasures of life, like a Sunday afternoon promenade and cinema. I knelt in front of the altar with other girls; we prodded each other and glanced at the rows of boys on the other side of the altar. After a year or two, I realised that the gap between the other girls and me was becoming wider.

I knew all the verses of religious songs better than anyone else anyway, thanks to Mařenka Žofáková, our cook, who loved me, and I her. I will never know why Mařenka did not enter a convent in her adolescence. It would have been so natural for her. Instead, she began working for us and stayed seventeen years, until she broke her arm and had to leave. Mařenka, who was referred to in Josefov as an old maid, had her own celestial world, her embroidery, and me. She liked Mother and Father as well, but she fussed especially over me – woke me up, put me to sleep, and grumbled at me when I didn't dress warmly enough in winter. She taught me all the religious songs and endless sentimental ballads such as 'On the edge of a German town, stands a beau-u-utiful castle on a rock ...' and she also drew me into her world of naive belief in goodness, love, God and all the saints. They were pretty fairy tales, and helped in my 'meeting' Violet.

I wrote all this to Violet and enclosed a star cut out from yellow linen, so that she could touch it, look at it and read the word JUDE. I had cut out the star myself from a large strip of strong linen. Half a centimetre from the thick black line of the star was a thin dotted line which had to be neatly tucked under. I had to cut around each point of the stars and tack them onto all our coats and dresses, to be worn whenever we were outside the house. My parents sat in front of me dumbfounded, as if it were they who were guilty and being judged. How could they begin, what could they say? Obviously, they explained it well; I felt no degradation; on the contrary I became defiant. 'Mother, please don't be embarrassed by the star, you'll see what I am going to do!'

Before anybody could stop me, I grabbed my coat with its star, and left the house. Everything had changed: the town, me, perhaps even the sky. As I have already said, the town of Josefov comprises a military fort and civilian houses. In each street you can see from one end to the other. The central street widens into a town square, a fountain in the middle, the square surrounded by a grove of chestnut trees and, beneath the chestnut trees, numerous benches, somewhere for the soldiers to sit with their girls. Near the fountain, I sat down on one of these benches. I sat there for quite a few hours inviting a challenge. I was possessed by anger and stubbornness. Until then, I had had the reputation of being 'a nice little girl'. At that moment, I certainly was not a nice little girl. I will show those Gestapo supporters, I repeated angrily to myself, again and again. So what? Was it just a pretence that, until now, people liked me and I them? But my challenging expression did not succeed. A few children said, 'Hi, come with us. What are you sitting there for? We're going to play cops and robbers on the ramparts.' An adult or two sat next to me and asked how things were at home. 'So you can see, Violet,' I wrote to my new friend, 'I wanted to challenge the world but no one responded!'

Since that afternoon, with my adolescence progressing in leaps and bounds, and since meeting Violet, much had changed. Now I even heard the cry, 'Wait, you Jewess, the Germans will fix you.' This insult, hurled by a former classmate of mine, did not hurt me too much. The whole town knew that Irena, with her dyed blonde hair, even though she was not yet fourteen, hung around the barracks and went out with German soldiers.

Violet offered me her friendship just at this time. It was an unselfish gesture and I was conscious of that. I had been behaving as if nothing were wearing me down, but in my heart, and in my diary, I had been asking many unanswerable questions of the human race and of God. And all at once, one insignificant person from the Sudeten border had detached herself from that 'humanity' and refused to conform. In a hateful and deadly time, full of suspicion and informers, she had held out her hand to me.

Our letters were full of descriptions of insignificant everyday happenings which alternated with reflections about the meaning of life. We even shared thoughts regarding the history of humanity and, well, just everything. Both of us asked questions which had remained unanswered since time immemorial. We were young and audacious, we knew little, but our thoughts were bold. Violet's search for the right answers was made easier by her strong yet simple and pure faith. Everything for her was in God's hands. God's will was the right will although godly paths might be unpredictable. But my childhood belief had gone. I bitterly argued with God. I reproached Him: 'If you existed, you would not allow the murdering of innocent people.' I even stopped going to church. Doubts about a perfect world began to appear between the lines of Violet's letters, particularly when I later wrote to her about more and more anti-Jewish decrees. The Nazis did not issue them at one time, but sadistically, one after the other – about school, parks, animals: which for me meant my dog Miki.

'My sister's husband is a big strong chap,' wrote Violet in a letter. 'Up until now he was always healthy, but recently he fell from a railway truck while loading wood. When they took him away, no one knew that it would all end with only a leg in plaster. When I saw how this person, otherwise as solid as a rock, became downcast and pitiful, how helplessly he leant on a stranger's shoulder, it occurred to me how quickly a person's fate can change. A fall from two metres high is enough ... enough ...

'Altogether, this week was too much for our little village. My friend's mother was buried: she had hanged herself. Even though we all know each other, or think we do (indeed there are just a few of us here and we care for one another), none of us knows *why* she did it. From childhood, we have tended cows, goats and sheep on the same meadows, and have chatted around a camp fire – about absolutely everything, I thought. But now it occurs to me do we really know everything about each other? What else remains hidden behind the tiny windows of our cottages? Even for our priest, perhaps? I always thought that our village solidarity distinguished us from the city. There, I think nobody cares for others. Here, even the most insignificant event is scrutinised in detail, and can ruffle the quiet waters. Maybe you will be critical: the fact that everyone worries about everyone else can simply be curiosity, words, gossip, pretentious interest. But I have always thought, if things got too difficult and someone really needed help, everyone would do all they could. Yet doubts flash across my mind. Perhaps I am wrong. Is it really like that? How is it in your town? Please, write your opinion about this to me, it worries me.'

As I do not have my letter, I don't know what I replied. But I was already more sceptical, so it was probably not too reassuring.

Christmas 1941 was approaching. Violet's Christmas letter said: 'Dear, you cannot imagine how much I am looking forward to Christmas. I am looking out of our cottage window, which frames a beautiful picture – the ground is dressed in a new garb. There is white all around, it sparkles, the nearby forest is sugar-coated. Christmas, Christmas – will you come soon? I am not only looking forward to it because there may be a present under the tree, but the many other things which Christmas signifies. In the front garden, the pine tree's boughs bend under the weight of snow, there is always lots here, and at dusk all of us will meet around the tree and sing carols. We make the Christmas decorations and know them well, but when we put them on the tree, it seems as if someone else placed them there, and as if human hands had not touched them. They are so mysterious and magical. Those moments around the tree, when we sing or are quiet, are never mundane. We have a small nativity set under the tree, which Grandfather carved. He was Mother's father whom I never knew. He was a glassmaker too, and died young from tuberculosis. Carved Baby Jesus is small and mild, and the presents around him are given with love. Here at home, the gifts are only little ones, but how much love and economy they represent. When one of us manages to really surprise the other, everybody lights up with pleasure – more than the candles on the tree.

'On Christmas Eve, we go to midnight Mass together and sing – my father, mother, brothers and sisters and me. We sing "Jesus Christ is born this day" and it feels as if we are all children again. It is true that during this period we are terribly dejected by the horrible situation and sad times but, momentarily, all that is forgotten. I want to believe that no one in the world is alone with their pain, and that during our time there are many others who have suffered and will suffer, but love and justice *must* eventually triumph!'

It was a plea for universal justice. Violet's faith in its fulfilment was shaken daily, and sometimes she had to fight against her own misgivings.

'What carefree days I had when I was little! It was so lovely, so serene to know nothing of the hatred and jealousy that exist in the adult world. Why can't we stay children? There is some sort of poison which infects people when they enter adulthood. Adults are simply unable to enjoy the little things that are around them. Why is that? I do not know how to explain it – it is as if each embodies oppression and guilt and they thrash around each other trying to appease that guilt. Unlike children, they are ashamed to be themselves, they pretend to enjoy "little things": the sun shining and warming the earth, or a beautiful ladybird flying high after a long winter ("Ladybird, Ladybird, fly away home, your house is on fire, your children alone"). Adults all seem so well informed, but are they really wise and cultured?'

All at once she was startled by her own reasoning and was alarmed by its pretentiousness. 'What a dumb-bell I am. I understand the problems of life to about the same extent as a goat understands roses, and I would like to change the world and think up something grand! Oh yes! At least you see how ignorant and devoid of common sense your new friend is. The people around me are probably right when they say, "Jarmila, Jarmila, whatever will come of your philosophising? Instead, you should learn to cook and sew properly ..." (they are right, I don't enjoy those tasks I must confess).'

I had her picture on the shelf by my bedhead: a girl with the face of a Madonna, like those in the colour pictures our priest gave us for attending Mass. My seemingly fragile friend actually operated machines in a Tanvald textile factory. The noise of the machines was as constant and far-reaching as the ideas of this unusually thoughtful girl. She keenly aspired to do something great and beautiful. She revelled in ideas, rebellion, longing and joy. All of this was in the letters which we regularly exchanged, at least once a week. I waited impatiently for hers. Because of our straight street, I could see the postman from my window when he appeared at one end. After so many years, when I recall those youthful but really such mature letters, I know now that Violet must have grown up quickly. She had no time. We had no time, neither she nor I. I do not have my letters to her, though I believe that she hid them in a secret place behind the beam in the attic where she lived and died. I know their contents only from Violet's responses.

Above all, we were both troubled by a big *why?* Why was there so much suffering: punishment without wrongdoing, wrongdoing without punishment? What was behind the concept of original sin and punishment? I have already said that Violet believed more unquestioningly than I. My childish trust had been deeply shaken. My cousin Bertie, a clever boy who could beat Grandfather at chess and was held up to me as an example of mathematical ability, was in the first Prague transport of Jews taken east. He was fifteen. He disappeared and with him his beautiful Viennese Jewish mother, my Aunt Paula. Grandmother's brother, Great-uncle Richard, such a lovely man, committed suicide ... I could go on, and on, and on. Concepts of good and evil, justice and truth, which my grandfather taught me by word and deed, had been shifted and twisted from their defined places. I was angry with God. I demanded answers. An increasing number of people exploited the situation – money-makers, flunkeys.

Violet answered my defiance: 'My dear! Thank you a thousand times for your impatiently awaited letter. What have I done to deserve your great trust? You are so good. My sorrowful friend, I do understand. I would like to help you so much in your anguish, but I see my own misery and shortcomings clearly. Despite everything, please rely on God's goodness, it is great. Dear Renée, you imagine that I am a sort of old-fashioned, devout, country girl. But no, not really. My belief is sometimes the only pillar I have, in this world full of anger and hatred. In trying times, the nation's mainstay used to be the country folk. But something strange has happened. This century of progress has affected the nation's soul and, in my opinion, not positively. What once was called the "pure and natural soul" of country people has disappeared. Even this village is full of those who laugh at everything which they previously held in awe. They ridicule and scorn us because we revere God's word.

'Let me describe one incident. The very day our Czechoslovakian Republic ceased to exist and when our beloved mountains were seized, our priest told us about the heritage of Saint Wenceslas. He confided to us that in the morning when he heard the news he cried and was desolate. Then, as usual, he had to take Mass. His thoughts gradually calmed down and he entrusted all to God. The wheels of history, he told us, do not always turn for the ease of mankind. How I wished that I could have known our priest better. He was such a good man and we were all his children. But now, that is not possible. Shortly after the occupation, he was arrested and now no one knows where he is. Sometimes I am fearful that even worse times could come. But even then, we must not submit or surrender!

'There is an old saying: "It was never so bad that it couldn't be worse!" We must learn to be patient and have faith. And even if we are shaken with despair by the evil which is all around us, we must not capitulate. I think that only love and mutual support can give us strength. Don't be cross, my dear, that I answer your letter with my own opinions. I say what I think, even if I am wrong. I am also frightened by the fact that some people quickly "change allegiance" while others are pressured to do so. Sometimes I think that the many people who indulged in excessive patriotism during the First Republic did so because it was fashionable, rather than through genuine feeling. And when patriotism becomes a fashion, then a sudden about-face hardly surprises anyone. Sincere love for one's homeland is deep, it lasts for ages and nothing can tear it apart. I believe there are many people who care about our country. They will remain linked together like a strong chain, outlasting all suffering, and, one hopes, some of them will live to experience a new blossoming of, and glory in, our country, where "water flows through the meadows, and pines rustle through the rocky cliffs" [the quotation is from the Czech national anthem]. The world continues to revolve and it won't stop, so we must hope that the sun's golden rays will shine again on our land. Perhaps, because of the suffering, our country will be enhanced, it will be more precious to us and we will value it even more. When our ancestors were most oppressed they sang: "Saint Wenceslas, don't allow us or our descendants to perish!"'

It was an impassioned letter, and by today's standards it seems old-fashioned and rhetorical. But Violet did not wish to move an audience to tears; she was just writing to one sad child. In their little cottage there was no one who could prompt or advise her. Anyway, no one had time. She wrote me things about which, in those days, others would not dare speak, they were too afraid. If Violet had also been afraid perhaps her fate would have been different. But that was not her nature. She would have always revealed herself and her beliefs. I think that if we two had not met on that chilly train she would, in any event, have met someone else who would have led her on a dangerous path.

Altogether, in evil times, those who overcome their own fear and by a seemingly insignificant step move humanity's conscience provide one of the reasons why life makes sense. Their deeds do not receive official recognition as heroic, no chronicler will record them, but it is because of their deeds that we need not be ashamed to call ourselves decent human beings.

One day a letter came from Violet which took my breath away.

'Sweetheart,' she wrote, 'I want to thank you for your lovely Christmas present and your letter, but I can't find the right words. I could jump for joy. But imagine – I can't even do that. After having been ill, I still feel tired and exhausted. I have a gift for you, too, and if things work out, I may be able to give it to you personally. I am quite bold, so I decided to accept your invitation. I am really looking forward to seeing you, only I am afraid that you may be disappointed. How will you find this ordinary, country girl, with no special talents or city sophistication? You must forgive the shortcomings of a not very notable person. I am not sure yet which day I will "dash off", but probably on St Stephen's [Boxing] Day. I will come by train, the one which leaves here at 7.30 a.m., and it would be wonderful if you could meet me.

'I have another favour to ask of you: could you also visit us? You know we have no idea what's happening in the world at the moment. We don't read the papers and our radio is being repaired. Can you come? Surely you are not guarded to such an extent that you would not be able to disappear for a few days? You are only little, nobody would notice you. You can't imagine how very glad we would all be! We all cordially invite you. My sister Daša would like to thank you personally for her present. Your beautiful gift almost knocked her off her feet, that's how pleased she was. If only events in the near future would repay all your generosity in kind! I wish you such happiness and joy because you are a comfort to all and give joy to others. One day, you must be recompensed for your suffering. You endure everything so patiently. "The wheel of fate" turns constantly, and one day truth will emerge and your current pain and misery will deepen your understanding of real happiness. I know that your dreams and ideals have been dashed, but perhaps beauty and splendour are not free and we have to struggle to perceive them? You will bear your own cross of pain to the end and you will be rewarded. And never, ever again make the assumption that I would prefer local girlfriends because of their "better pedigree"! Never for a moment should you think that!'

(I do not know what it was I had felt and written, to which this was an answer. Presumably I had been jealous.)

Around noon, Violet got off the train. It was freezing and snow crunched beneath our feet. There was hardly a soul in the street and that was a good thing. We were silent, both of us reserved and feeling awkward, barely glancing at each other's eyes. The path from the station to the Josefov military fort crosses three bridges. It takes about twenty minutes.

My home, to which I led Violet, was not like my home of old. As I have explained, the first step towards the loss of privacy which would become complete in the concentration camp was the relocation of several Jewish families to our apartment. But, even with this arrangement, I still had my own room, although it was now also used as our living and dining room. There, I had my own bed, a shelf with my books, and my hiding places in the small writing desk. Violet and I, hand in hand, entered through the front door, which still carried a copper name plate with my father's name, Richard Fries, on it.

Fortunately, time stopped for the next two beautiful days. Minutes became hours. From our letters we knew a lot about each other, but now! There was so much to talk about. Violet was enchanted by the festively decorated table (unfamiliar to her), by further gifts that waited for her family and herself beneath the Christmas tree, by the copper utensils on the kitchen walls, by the old chest and the paintings. I played a Schubert Impromptu on the piano for her, which, as a Christmas present for Mother, I had learnt by heart. That same day, I took her to my secret 'cave' in the ramparts where, behind a two-hundred-year-old wall in a dark passage, I had a hideaway for my most valued treasures. We made a little fire there and, until darkness fell, divulged our secrets to each other. No one could hear us, high on the ramparts above the houses, but we still whispered because we were not used to such intimacies.

'Mr Vašíček' – Violet, writing to me later, did not even dare to use the Christian name of this 'older man' – 'is twenty. He's an adult and should know better, yet he behaves like a little boy. He works at the same factory among all the girls. Why did he have to eye me off?' demanded Violet disdainfully, but I realised how pleased she really was. He would love to take her dancing, or to a fair. He said his feelings were genuine and he was quite serious, and he even wanted to ask permission from Violet's mother. I was delighted that she, a young lady, was consulting me, a mere girl, about matters of love. I had a great time moralising, though perhaps it was sour grapes on my part – I liked boys and I was even 'in love' with a matriculation student. But I was only fourteen and, besides, the situation was too difficult. Why did she take my young, puritan opinion so seriously? I said she should show him the door, she was too young to get married, she had plenty of time for boys. She sincerely thanked me for my 'advice'. My dear Violet did not know that time for her was completely lacking. I do not know what happened with Mr Vašíček and I only hope that at least somewhere, some time, they kissed. How captivated he must have been by that delicate, slender nymph with wavy, long, light autumnal-brown hair, an oval-shaped face, a classically straight nose, large blue eyes and thick, long, blonde eyelashes. Mr Vašíček did not know how bad an adviser Violet chose concerning matters of the heart. On top of that, we were both enthralled by nineteenth-century Czech writers: Karolina Světlá, Eliška Krásnohorská. Krásnohorská's novel *Queen of the Bluebells* was our model for romantic relationships. It took years before I extricated myself from those influences but time was denied to Violet.

How differently I should advise now! It might be something like: 'My dear, each love may be the last, each day the last one, go and live this day, go and live your love! Do whatever gladdens your heart, listen to no one. It's not easy in your village, since people stare into every nook and cranny, and they follow everyone's movements from behind the dainty curtains of their windows. But, even so, try and experience joy or, at least, flashes of happiness. That will be good and right.'

But at that time, I did not know that, nor did she. Violet could not behave naturally, as she was influenced by the fear of gossip. She both wanted to behave decently and had done so. For a respectable village girl it was the accepted code. Mr Vašíček, 'that green boy with a childlike face' as she once described him, infiltrated her letters for quite a while. Her attachment to this tall, skinny boy with a serious face was deeper than she actually wanted to admit. Neither of them knew what to do. When 'Mr Vašíček' tried to court another girl, Violet commented 'thank goodness'. For three months he managed to avoid their workshop, did not accompany her to the train, ignored her. Violet 'sighed with relief'. But one day, when work finished, he appeared in front of the factory and, without asking, joined her and said: 'I want to change my life for you, I can't live without you.'

Even then, she rejected him. He was sad and introspective, she wrote. It was too much for her, she could not think about anything other than his sad face. When he approached her again and said, 'On Sunday, I am coming to your village. Meet me at the station, I must definitely speak to you, whether you want to or not!' Violet rebuffed him and did not go. She hesitated but then wrote to me: 'He's very serious about me. Now, I'm really frightened what will happen to me because of this. I think I am really awful to him. It is left to God's mercy ...'

Violet continued her letter the next day. 'He came to work looking serious and sad. I expected him to reproach me for not coming. But nothing. He didn't even look at me. I began feeling sorry for his sadness, and I wanted to apologise. But how? I didn't have the nerve to go to him. I wrote two lines of an apology and discreetly put it on his machine. "Please don't be angry, I couldn't come yesterday." By the same means, two days later, I received his reply. He troubled my conscience and was apparently waiting for a reply. I handed him the next letter personally. He wrote to me once again. The day after, he waited in front of the factory gate and, without asking, he joined me. Frankly, I could not forbid this as he lives near the station and went this way anyhow.'

Fancy Violet apologising! 'But he didn't say anything silly and you know what? He persuaded me to meet him. We went to a fair in Držkov with Mrs Válková from my village. I hope it's not so bad. Surely this sort of friendship can't harm me?'

'To tell the truth,' Violet continued, 'it was that lady's doing, you know. On the way, we chatted about everything under the sun. I hadn't felt so happy in ages. Perhaps we will become good friends. I don't think I love him that much.' Violet was still defensive towards me and herself. 'He really is a nice boy. He doesn't talk about anything that might upset me and each day we stroll from the factory together so at least I don't have to walk alone in the dark. Sometimes we chat at lunchtime. Usually he sews something during this break and I go over to him with the other girls (they all like him around here) to gossip. Maybe we'll go to the fair in Držkov again tomorrow, if it's not raining.'

In her next letter there was unexpected news. 'Perhaps we'll soon be able to talk together, as I'm hoping to visit you! I'm not sure if you know that my sister Manka moved to Hradec Králové and she isn't well and is in hospital. I could combine a hospital visit with a visit to your house. I am terribly keen to see you. I'll show you a photo of Mr Vašíček which he gave me. I hope I'll find you alive and well, it will be delightful. The whole family greets you, and I especially.'

The words 'I hope I'll find you alive' would have sounded absurd at any other time, but in that summer of 1942 they were quite normal. It was the year of transports and Violet knew about these things from me. Any day a communiqué could come, to 'go there and there with 50 kilograms of luggage', and within a week we could disappear. Our Prague relatives gradually disappeared to somewhere in the east. Where? No one knew exactly. The Germans were successful in cultivating uncertainty and a general lack of information regarding deportations. Consequently, rumours spread among us and even when the transports began, the word *east* reeked of smoke, incineration and horror. Of course, everybody clung to the term 'work transport' as a lifebuoy. They had to, in order to survive. Soon they were whispering the word *gas*. Apparently this word was discreetly marked on form letters from inmates of the concentration camps at Auschwitz and Maidanek.

'Impossible, it can't be true, we live in the twentieth century,' they said.

'Oh yes, we are sure they are taking us to work, that is still true. There's a war, but gas? No! It is unthinkable!'

Unfortunately, it was not.

At this, our third meeting, Violet and I once again hugged each other.

She brought a basketful of sweet-smelling, juicy blueberries. When she picked them, she had prayed that fate would spare us. Belatedly, we celebrated my fifteenth birthday. That year my Maytime birthday was as lovely as ever. For me, it will always be associated with the scent of peonies and the tender, spring-green leaves of silver birches. In spite of this, my birthday was different, utterly different. Custom-made ship's bags stood in the corner of the room, at hand and ready to be filled with whatever we were permitted to take with us when the doors of our home were finally shut. My childhood birthdays, which seemed so distant now, had been spent in Mnichovo Hradiště with my grandparents and were always merry. Grandpa established the 'tradition': on the morning of *the day* I was woken up by the sound of wooden spoons banging against some pots, while lids were struck one against the other and neighbours and girl friends, all in fancy dress, marched in and pulled me out of bed. Together we tramped around the house and garden. It ended with a sumptuous breakfast.

Now, in 1942, Grandfather arrived sad and worried. We all thought about Grandmother who was alone and abandoned in that big building. We knew nothing of our future, nor did we know that Violet's meeting with my grandfather would be fateful for both of them.

Violet left the next day, Grandfather the day after that. In letters from Prague, Uncle Vilík implored me: 'Times are harsh, strive to support your parents, be bright and sunny, more than you have been in the past.' I tried, but it was terribly difficult. I did not really succeed. I wrote bitter complaints in my diary about my parents' bad moods and I could not tell myself that it was my fault, at least not always; it had to be the times. Unfortunately I fulfilled the role of an unwitting scapegoat.

One of the last letters I had from Violet was a response to our daily worsening situation. 'I think about you every day and it hurts me to know how unhappy you must be. Last week you wrote that each day you expect to relinquish your home. It grieves me so, that I can't even express it. I can't imagine that. Believe me, my heart goes out to you. I feel how dreadful it must be, to live in such awful uncertainty and know that the moment will come when you must part with everything that, until now, has formed your life and home.

'I think about you and sometimes feel so intensely, as if it were happening to me. What will happen tomorrow, and the day after that? And then what? What will become of us all? I don't know, and perhaps that's better. If the future is going to be a happy one and we are here to see it, our joy will be even greater after experiencing this suffering. And if our future is to be unhappy, then it's better that we know nothing! Like this, at least some sparks of hope remain. And as long as we hope, we can live. They say a handful of certainty is better than a sackful of hope, but in this case the saying does not apply. Certainty could be so awful that it would be horrible to know what lies ahead.

'No, I can't even think about it. We mustn't increase our worries – we all have a lot but your family has even more. Forgive me, my dear Renée, that I bother you with my sad reflections, I should write something more cheerful to make you happy. But I can't, my head swirls with gloomy thoughts.'

A week later, 'I must tell you what is happening to me. After reading your letter, I was horrified that maybe we wouldn't be able to see each other again and, without warning or asking, I wanted to turn up. But on Saturday any possibility of travelling became unthinkable. I became ill. For some time now, I have had a cough and headaches. I didn't pay much attention to them but on Friday I decided to go to the doctor. He assured me that it was nothing but that I should stay at home for a few days. That suited me, I wanted to meet you and visit my sister in Hradec Králové.

'Lately, I have been constantly tired, almost exhausted, and so those eight days felt like a gift from heaven. But this pleasant break didn't turn out well. I am really sick. I am coughing, maybe I have the flu, and something is wrong with my throat. For five days I have had a fever. I can't even go to the doctor. I am registered with one in the Sudetes mountains, in Velké Hamry, and it's too far for me, I wouldn't make it. So the surprise which was to be my journey to you has come to nothing. It's a complete muddle. I didn't even have the strength to answer your sad letter immediately.

'As soon as I am a little better, I will come straight away. Only don't be taken away from me before then. I only ever have two days off, but I must see you!

'I have to finish. I am terribly hot, in spite of mother saying it's cold in here. I am tired and there is no reason why. Everyone greets you, even our smallest, five-year-old Kamil. Please give my regards to your parents and don't forget to send me a photo of you. Give Betulinka and little Jiříček a kiss. I so wish that these horrible times could be at an end and you wouldn't have to fear for your home. One

more kiss – God keep you safe, sweet girl. We are in His hands and we must believe that He will not abandon us!
'With good wishes and goodnight, your friend Jarmila.'
It was a sad letter, full of anxiety and a diminishing belief that 'God will not abandon us'. Perhaps Violet's illness weakened her rock-solid faith that 'God's will is the right will'.
But the illness was not influenza. As I learned long after the war, it was the family's scourge, the 'glassmaker's illness', tuberculosis.

Let's go back to Betulinka and Jiříček whom Violet greeted. Their story deserves to be sung in a drawn-out, wailing Jewish song, such is its tragedy. Neither their story nor their names are fictitious and the two children lit up the dark sky of war like meteorites. They shone and they were obliterated. But before that our paths crossed. How?
I have mentioned the young family with two children who were moved into our home. They were the Feldmanns. Miriam was young and beautiful, with eyes like deep, endless pools. Her husband, Moses, was as thin and tall as a beanstalk, with a big nose and spectacles which always slipped down to its tip. At that time I was not familiar with the name of the Yiddish writer Sholom Aleichem or his stories about poor Jews from eastern Europe but much later I learned that he took his examples of poor tailors and shopkeepers from real life. Moses (Moishe) Feldmann was one such. He and Miriam spoke Yiddish, similar to German but interspersed with Polish and Russian words, which my father understood a little. They quickly adopted a few Czech words. Their two children, four-year-old Betulinka and eighteen-months-old Jiříček, picked up Czech easily, of course.
The family of four lived with us, across the passage in our former office, which we helped furnish with basic necessities. They were content, since they came from such poverty that they appreciated any comfort. For me, they were mysterious and interesting. Miriam, with her ivory-white complexion framed by black ringlets, often visited our kitchen, which became like a common room. She used to sit on a stool in the corner, both children under her wing, and sing. She sang songs which I had not heard then, in a language I did not know, but which I somehow understood. They were songs about the suffering of Jewish mothers whose children had been taken by Cossacks and spiked onto fences, songs about sadness and the death of their – and now our – ancestors. Those songs could only have been in a minor key and

45

brought tears to my eyes. One was a lullaby 'leila la leila ...' Never again, not even in the ghetto, did I hear Jewish songs sung so movingly.

More than once Miriam would be daydreaming, her head resting on her shoulder, crooning her songs in the kitchen, when Moishe would fly in. He screeched rather than shouted, 'Home! Where do you think you belong, woman? With me, move!'

It was said in that strange tongue, but it had to have some such meaning. I had never seen such behaviour towards a woman, it was new to me. Without annoyance, compliantly and politely, she got up and went with him. Why doesn't she resist, I thought to myself. I would not tolerate such treatment! Sometimes she clung crying onto the doorhandle of our apartment, one hand ringing the bell, and when someone opened the door she would beg us to hide her from her Moishe who had got out of bed on the wrong side and maybe would beat her to death. We would let her in and then Moishe would bang on the door and yell, 'What's it got to do with you, my wife and me? She won't sleep with me and it's her duty in the eyes of God. I have my conjugal rights!'

She stayed with us until the racket on the door ceased. Quiet followed, and only Jiříček's feeble sobs broke the silence. She would straighten out her clothes, smooth down her hair, wipe her tears and leave. Nothing further would be heard. She probably quietened Jiříček and nurtured him from her big white breast, then more than likely calmed Moishe down and embraced him.

Mother made every effort to shield me from this strange couple's exotic sex life. She did not succeed. Miriam regarded me as an adult and also as a trusted confidante to whom she could whisper her intimate secrets. I learnt quite a lot, so much so that I had plenty to forget in *my* later sex life. Among other things, that cries and beatings went hand in hand with the passionate fusion of their bodies. 'He loves me,' she whispered to me. 'He could torture me to death.' How dreadful it was, but how thrilling. We used to sit together on the bottom step leading down to the cellar. She hid there from her husband, I from my mother, father and all the other residents who regarded themselves as my protectors from the Feldmanns.

One night – arrests always happened at night – the Gestapo banged on the door and we were all dragged from our beds, but eventually they took away only Moishe and Miriam. No one knew why. It was rumoured that Moishe Feldmann had stolen some potatoes from a field.

Well, he fed four mouths and rations for Jews were less than for others, so it is possible.

Passionate, gaunt Moishe and beautiful Miriam's two children stayed behind. What could we do with them? Who was able to look after small children here? And what would happen to them when there was a transport? The adults agreed that they had enough problems of their own. 'We shall place the children with the Jewish Council, there is surely a Jewish orphanage, nothing else can be done, they have to go.' Those who made these statements were riddled with guilt. But honestly, what *could* be done? Little Jiříček was still breast-fed. Really, nothing could be done. And, anyway, even if Moishe did steal those potatoes, the offence was not so grave as to prevent their being released and then collecting their children from the orphanage. The game that 'everything will turn out well' was a deep-rooted exercise.

After that council-of-war decision regarding the children, I could not sleep. The following day, I walked around like a shadow and towards evening approached Mother.

'Mama, we all know that the children will be separated, and yet they belong together. You know how much Miriam loved them, how nice and good they are. Mama, I'll look after them in my room, no one will know a thing!'

I met stubborn resistance but I also felt her wavering. To the question 'And what of your studies, your other duties?' I hastily argued, 'It's so chaotic in the flat that I'm not studying anyway. I'll easily clean up the two remaining rooms in the morning and, as always, I'll light the fire in the kitchen stove and make breakfast. Mama dear, I'm not giving the children to anybody.'

So the children stayed with me, they loved me and I them, madly. Their trust gave me back my confidence. They were well behaved, too well behaved. Perhaps my memory fails me, but I cannot recall that they ever made me angry or that they ever were unmanageable. My 'human dolls' were cleaner and happier by the day. In the closed world of adults, where hardly anyone went out, and where mostly sad and anxious conversations were carried on, I lived a completely different and separate life with 'my' children. Betulinka and Jiříček knew nothing about the word 'war', nothing about transports, nothing about the fact that the east they came from had become a different 'east' and probably meant death for the Jews. They did not know the meaning of being a Jew, any more than German-born children of a similar age knew the meaning of being *Herrenvolk* (gentry). They laughed the same way as all children in this world, with unspoilt, clear, ringing peels of laughter. Until the transport, I lived with them in a fantastic fairy-tale world, without deception and full of spontaneous fun. I think that we all benefited from having the children around. Our tiny community was thrilled when Jiřík elatedly brought in his potty, proud of what he had done. Betulinka helped dry the dishes, made Jiřík's and her bed, and learnt how to play 'Baa Baa Black Sheep' on the piano. She sang well and taught me some lullabies which her mother used to whisper in her ear. Betulinka would not see adulthood to sing her mother's songs. 'My children' perished when I was fifteen years old. I was old enough to experience the deep pain of having them taken away. Never, ever, have I accepted their loss.

So ends the wailing song.

After the memorable Christmas of 1941, it was several months before we saw Grandfather again. He came in May 1942 and then again in August. In the evening, Grandfather and I would walk through the fields behind our house. The track was wide and I held onto Grandfather's hand like a leech. I was overcome by sadness and joy. Grandfather would be silent for quite a while and I dared not break that silence. I had learnt to live with an unchildlike load of adult worries during those difficult times. Then Grandpa began to speak in his melodic voice.

'There's nothing in the world I wouldn't do, my sweetheart, to protect you from what you must live through. But it's beyond my control to exchange my life for yours, and alter where life has placed you. The only advice I can give is to remind you how great a solace Nature is: time, space – infinite and noble – which again and again renew life. Look above you. The August sky is the most beautiful.

'Can you see? A falling star. Make a wish, it will come true. And there, another one, and another.' And then he pointed out the constellations Cassiopeia, the Big and Little Dippers, Berenice's Locks. 'In January, the heavens look as bright and the stars shine just the same as today. I won't point out any more, you won't remember them. Next time, in January.'

But there would be no visit from my grandfather in the following January. By then, my parents and I would be gone, travelling to an unknown destination.

I have three postcards that Violet sent during that last period before transportation. On one is the Prague Christ child resembling Betulinka. On the second (sent from the fair) is the commemorative plaque which is on the birthplace of the Czech writer Antal Stašek (1843–1931). On the last one is a mountain cottage set on a snowy slope and dated 12 December 1942. 'This photo looks like winter at our house in the mountains,' she wrote.

Then we were summoned to the transport. The Hradec Králové region was to have its turn. There were three numbered tags enclosed with the summons: CH 16, CH 17 and CH 18, mine. The tags were made out of strong cardboard so they would last. We had to string them around our necks, and from that moment names were irrelevant; we were just numbers. This 'game', which was supposed to end well, had a new twist: it was becoming more complicated.

I wrote all this to Violet. Her reply came immediately. In Jesenný, the whole family was gathered at home and 'everyone, but everyone, implores you, my dear Renuška, not to join the transport. My parents beseech your parents to allow us to take you under our protection. We have all carefully considered this. There are so many of us in the cottage that you will safely see the war out. It is the end of 1942, it can't last much longer! If necessary, there's a hideout under the sloping roof behind the attic room ready for you. We all beg you not to refuse our offer!!!'

Our family also held a secret meeting. The answer was a resounding no – we could not accept this. It was the most noble offer we had ever received but it was not feasible. If Heydrich had not been assassinated, perhaps we could have considered it. But now, when people are shot even for trivial matters, the discovery of hiding a transport escapee would result in the deaths of the whole Holat family. Mother wrote: 'We will remember your offer until our dying breath, and we thank you.'

A telegram with three words came: 'Pleading–Much–Holats'.

But, already, we had carefully weighed every possession and had chosen only essential items, those which were vitally necessary. My scouting experience paid off at this time. I had packed bags and rucksacks for everyone. Nothing protruded, and each was filled to capacity.

Early on the morning of 19 December (my parents' seventeenth wedding anniversary) our small group walked despondently through the quiet town to the Josefov-Jaroměř railway station to board the train that would take us to a school in Hradec Králové, the collection point, before being transferred to the ghetto-town of Terezín. There, a very different chapter of my life began.

From then until May 1945 I knew nothing more about Violet. Even now, I only know fragments of stories from a few well-informed people about the later years of Violet's life. It seems as if she dedicated her life to me and to those I loved. Perhaps she was obsessed by the desire to make amends for her sense of guilt over the fact that she stayed behind, and her friend had to go. She performed possible and impossible feats to help. She established contact with my uncle Vilík, who, so far, had remained free. She was not to know that he would be arrested. Denounced by a colleague who worked in the underground, he would be tortured in the Peček Palace. He was later taken to Pankrác prison, then to Buchenwald.

Violet wrote to my grandparents in Mnichovo Hradiště: she wanted to come and speak to them. She went. I am convinced that she had to use tact and consummate skill to convince them that she must be allowed to help us. Grandpa and Grandmother were people who would not risk someone else's life rather than their own.

Together they must have found the least dangerous scheme. For a while, it was possible to send to the Terezín concentration camp, where the three of us were, half-kilogram parcels of food, soap, toothpaste and other things. Uncle Vilík mobilised friends in Prague and they collected empty cigarette cartons labelled with the brand name *Abadia*, into which the half-kilogram of supplies could fit. He found a bookbinder who put false bottoms in the boxes and in these he sent us letters full of optimism and hope. In this way we learnt that the German troops had been defeated at Stalingrad in January 1943.

Every week, Father, Mother and I received a small parcel containing cubes of thickening, butter caramels, a piece of meat baked inside a small loaf of home-made bread, and some ship's biscuits. Among those who were still 'outside', recipes were circulated to prepare food that had the least volume and contained the most calories.

Because Mnichovo Hradiště is a small town, it was conspicuous to post such a large number of parcels addressed to Terezín. It could occur to each and everyone: what was the councillor sending in them? Probably food – what else to a concentration camp? And if food, from where? Surely his rations were insufficient? In short, it was dangerous.

The discovery of a hoard of food could mean prison, and perhaps death. So a portion of food went to my uncle in Prague, and his friends became part of the whole business. For that matter, parcels were not only sent to us. Many others waited for them too, and Vilík, Grandfather and Grandmother found a mission in preparing and sending the parcels. Violet also became involved in this chain but I do not know how often.

I can picture my gentle friend coming to the Mnichovo Hradiště railway station, if possible in the darkness of evening. Wrapped up in a woollen coat, she stealthily walks through unlit streets. She quickens her step at each sound. The mountains and valleys around her cottage did not frighten her, because there she walked on familiar, well-trodden tracks. But what about the person who disappeared around the corner, did he see her? Did he see her for the first time, or had he noticed her previously? Is he following her? Quickly she runs downhill past the church, along the last risk-laden street, and slips into the house at 80 Arnold Street, the house built by my real grandfather, Adolf Bondy, in 1910.

Who could have known that the informer lived in the house itself?

No doubt she closed the heavy oak doors quietly, then ran up the spiral staircase and turned 'my' doorknob. How Grandfather and Grandmother would have hugged Violet in their arms! They identified her with everything that connected us to them. They lived to do anything that would help to prolong our life and she joined in their efforts. How dear she was to them. Sometimes, probably, she slept at their house, so that she could return home in the early morning light. Did she sleep in my bed? I am sure that she adored my grandparents, it could not have been otherwise, and she had every reason to love them. She would have embraced the harmonious atmosphere which my grandparents had built up over decades. Grandpa Sieger was an avid collector of inlaid furniture, old chests and armaments, pewter plates and jugs, pictures and Meissen porcelain – there was everything. Perhaps during the evening the sound of the Viennese grand piano reverberated through the quietened house. Perhaps Grandpa and Violet sang? I am convinced that they did. It was better to make music than indulge in sadness and recollections. And my dear ones, the three of them, followed wise precepts: as long as you live, live by the best ideals and do your utmost for others.

Violet must have felt comfortable in the civilised atmosphere of my grandparents' home. How much this remarkable girl would have asked my grandfather, the judge and exemplar of justice in Mnichovo Hradiště. Surely she posed question after question, and just as surely he answered according to the dictates of his conscience. Apparently Violet went in and out of there for about six months. Each week during those six months she heaved a bag of parcels and distributed them around the post offices in Tanvald, Železný Brod ... For six months Father, Mother and I continued to receive small parcels in Terezín, filled with such love, without suspecting Violet's involvement. Each parcel was preceded by a printed card 'call for ...' The Germans maintained order in everything, and the Jewish Council they had set up ran according to their rules.

In the early months of 1943 Terezín experienced its most dreadful winter. Cruel frosts added to the misery. There were about 60,000 people in the small town. They came only in transit, but some stayed. At that time we were among the latter. We dreamed about home as one dreams of a safe oasis, but all the while the tragedy was creeping inexorably closer.

Suddenly, the parcels stopped. We did not know why. Alarmed, we speculated about what had happened. After a while, bad news reached us through mother's secret channel, a Czech policeman. It was a channel I had only suspected. Apparently Grandmother had been the first to be arrested, Grandfather staying free a short while longer. My grandmother was taken to Mladá Boleslav by the Gestapo. It was not until after the war that Mother and I found out that Grandfather and Vilík did everything they could to save her. They bribed somebody in the Gestapo, who promised ...

Violet was the next to be arrested, and shortly afterwards it was Grandfather's turn.

The denunciation made to the Gestapo in Mladá Boleslav had been signed by a resident of Mnichovo Hradiště. It was someone who knew our apartment well. 'They sent food to Jews in a concentration camp, they must have supplies. That old Jewess stood on the balcony outside the kitchen and abused the great German Empire and cursed Hitler.'

The Germans went straight to the supplies. During a house search they found them in the false ceiling of the bathroom. It turned out that our safe haven, protected by Grandpa's position, had been exposed by

a miserable shopkeeper, Mr H., the ground-floor tenant of our building, who only months earlier had boisterously banged pot lids on my
birthday.

What did Mr H. want? A trousseau for one of his still-small
children? Pictures? Chests? I don't know. He did not get much anyway.
Apparently the Gestapo came in a truck and took nearly everything
away. In June 1945, surprisingly soon after the war, when Mother and
I entered this man's apartment, Grandmother's curtains still hung on
the windows. On the table were cherries in an all too familiar hand-
cut glass bowl. At that time we still knew nothing of his treachery, but
Mother raised her eyebrows questioningly. 'Yes, yes,' he stammered
to me, 'your grandmother gave it to us well before her arrest, she was
such a nice lady. You know, we did so much for her and your grandfather.' We thanked him. Mama and I wanted nothing – we suspected
that these were the coveted 'things' which, most of all, had led to the
arrests.

Grandmother and Violet saw each other again in a women's prison
near Jičín. After the war, we gained a few fragments of information
about their lives from another inmate.

'Yes, they often encountered each other – that small, plump lady
(plump even then) and the thin, tall girl. We could all see how significant the contact was. They embraced and kissed with their eyes. We
were ordered to keep our eyes fixed to the ground, but who could
police the eyes of so many women? That old lady, your grandmother,
was always clean and tidy, her grey hair neatly patted down.'

Yes, that could not have been anyone other than my dear grandmother; she always wore a hair net and very probably was wearing it
when she was arrested.

'She behaved,' continued the woman, 'how can one say it? with
such dignity, perhaps even nobility. She walked with a quiet, resigned
step around the prison yard and, in spite of her silence, she made us
feel calm and in control of ourselves. I am sure everyone was fond of
her and from the day she ceased to attend the regular exercise sessions
we missed her very much.

'I missed her very, very much,' the woman repeated. 'Was that girl
a relative of yours? I said to myself she must be the old lady's grand-
daughter. In a sort of spiritual way they were very similar – not in
looks or build but in their expression and attitude regarding our circumstances. If she was your sister she was wonderful. I heard that she

was released from prison a few weeks before the end of the war because she was ill. I don't know. Her cheeks looked as if they were made up but otherwise she was skin and bone. Sometimes she was so weak that she couldn't even go out to the yard.

'I actually stayed in that prison until the end of the war. And what about you? Where were you? Did you meet up with your grandmother and your sister?'

No, we never saw Grandmother again. She faced a terrible path to death. But my 'sister', my dearest 'sister', yes, she and I did meet again. Only, that meeting comes later in the story.

Above
My grandparents'
house in Mnichovo
Hradiště.
Right
My mother with
my grandfather
Jan Sieger, in
1942.

Above left
*My grandmother
Františka and my dog
Miki.*
Above right
*My father Richard
Fries, in 1917.*
Left
*Uncle Vilík Bondy in
1938.*

Right
My parents in 1942.
Below
On my thirteenth birthday,
26 May 1940.

An outing with my father near Josefov, 1941.

With my father in 1942, after his imprisonment by the Gestapo.

18. 9. 1940. v Josefově.

Tento denník jsem dostala již dávno, ale dlouho jsem se nemohla rozhodnouti začíti si vésti denník. Psaním denníku získávám opravdu přítele s kterým si mohu popovídat dle libosti a který nic neprozradí. Milý příteli denníku, měl by si šťastnou přítelkyni kdyby... ...kdyby nebyly tak těžké doby jako jsou nyní. Jest mi 13 let a něco přes 3 měs. Začalo to dnem <u>15. března 1938</u>. Toho dne obsadili naši zemi Němci a čím dál a dál to jest horší. Nyní, jelikož jsem neárijka nesmím chodili do školy ani do biografu. Můj tatínek teď dostal do obchodu komisaře a jsou s maminkou pořád rozčileni (čemuž se ani nedivím) a já to někdy odnesu. Vyučuji se nyní doma a učí mě jeden náš známý, pan Winternitz, s kterým se pořád hádám. Udělal mi celodenní rozvrh, podle kterého se mám říditi. Včera mi bylo strašně, strašně

The first entry in my diary, 18 September 1940.

Above
*Myself and Violet,
1942.*
Left
*At home with
Betulinka.*

My yellow star.

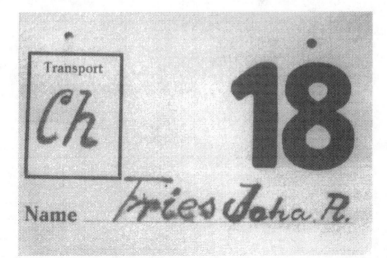

My transport number.

The march from Bohušovice to Terezín.

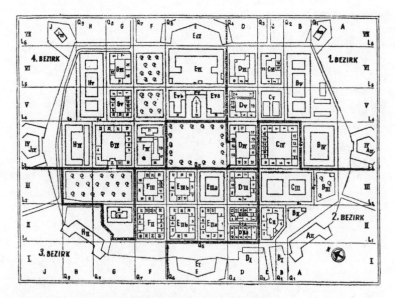

Renamed streets of the Terezín ghetto.

Towards the unknown

Smells are the most important and splendid sensation during the weeks before Christmas: vanilla-flavoured icing sugar, muscatels, ginger, walnuts, almonds and sultanas. Place these delicacies in a hot oven and heavenly smells emanate from it. Loaves of Christmas sweet bread are carefully, almost sacredly, taken out of the oven. They haven't burnt? There is a hurried but pleasant nervousness about secretly tasting the delicacies, the sweeter the better.

Even during the weeks before the Christmas of 1942 the baking was done, but from completely different recipes. Recipes were always handed down from generation to generation, and from place to place. These particular recipes, however, circulated among those Jewish families expecting summons to the transport. Those recipes with the least volume but the most calories were the favourites – ship's biscuits and butter caramels made into the shapes of Christmas biscuits. A mixture of butter and flour was formed into fish, trees, dolls and birds.

It was known that the Hradec Králové transport, for which we were listed, would depart some time just before Christmas Eve. And it did. Two rooms, which had remained ours after other Jewish families from Jaroměř had been moved into our apartment, were full of things and heaped with our luggage. We tripped over each other, wondering again and again what or what not to take. The permitted weight of 50 kilograms seemed large enough, especially considering that we would have to carry it. There had to be room for everything: winter and summer clothes, a pillow, linen, a blanket, several pairs of shoes, toiletries, writing needs – in short, everything (as far as we could imagine) without which we could not exist. We knew that whatever was forgotten would be forgotten for good. Or if not for good, then for how long? How long would the war last? The opinions about time were absolutely individual and depended on the optimism or pessimism of each person.

It took a long time for us to prepare ourselves for that moment. We learned from other districts that the time between receiving the chit of paper which advised the date of departure and the actual departure of the transport was usually only one or two days. Naturally we had been preparing for a long time. I am sure that each one of us, Father, Mother, the other members of our involuntary 'community' and I, tried to imagine what lay ahead. As it happened, nothing in our imagination could even remotely match the reality. And now, in this December week, it was here.

It was the last evening at home. We packed. My scouting experience in packing rucksacks was also useful for the large ship's sacks which, on the advice of others, we had had sewn. I put the softest clothes towards the back and piled them up, so that as many as possible took up the least space. My parents knew that I was doing this well and that it was really up to me to cope. I was glad I didn't have to think about the forthcoming days.

For this last evening meal at home we had schnitzel and potato salad, a Christmas Eve meal ahead of time. We set up a festive table in my bedroom, the room that was now used for our daily life. Our largest hand-cut crystal bowl was placed conspicuously in the middle of the white tablecloth, and was filled with peaches and pineapples. We did not care if the bowl were broken. What difference would that make? There were also champagne glasses and a bottle of champagne. From time to time Mother said to help ourselves, surely we did not want to leave food for 'them'? But she, like Father and I, nibbled mechanically and, with a tight throat, swallowed the tasty food with difficulty. Such a Lucullan feast in the fourth year of the war! The meal was part of our emergency rations taken out from their hiding place, a recess behind a bookcase in the bedroom.

Father even poured me some champagne as a toast to our safe return. This was most unusual because, until then, I had not been allowed to drink anything alcoholic. Father was very concerned about the accessibility of liqueurs and wine which he produced and sold. He did not suspect that I knew the hiding place for the key to the cupboard in our elegant drawing room – now occupied by a family of four – and that I sometimes went there and sipped eggnog. When I told Father my secret he didn't get angry, he only smiled ruefully.

We finished that silent feast and, as usual, I washed the dishes. The table had been cleared. Only three sets of keys remained on it. According to the regulations, we had to take these with us and hand them in, otherwise we would be punished.

We had never moved house – neither my grandparents in Mnichovo Hradiště nor my parents in Josefov. They were not simply apartments but homes completely fashioned to our needs. Over the years, each object had its unmistakable place, even the mousetrap. I hated that ghastly invention. It is awful to trap a mouse with something it cannot resist and then kill it just before it can taste the aromatic bacon. The thought ran through my mind that we were entering a similar trap, on the vague promise that our family would remain together. The promise was that we would live, in a different place and in a different way, but live. Even though I had always been a trusting child and nobody had ever really deceived me, I did not believe this. And if *I* felt doubtful, what were my parents thinking?

I finished packing, changing things here and there for something which seemed more important. Occasionally, I took a thin slice of juicy pineapple and popped it in my mouth. I did this regardless of whether I wanted it or not: I just did not want someone strange touching the fruit tomorrow, or the day after. The error in comparing us with a mouse is that the mouse experiences euphoria and goes to its death without suspicion. But what about our suspicions?

We had to leave home at about three in the morning, so that in the darkness we would not miss the prescribed train to Hradec Králové. Common sense prevailed and we went to bed. But did any of us sleep? I don't know. They were our last hours, minutes, at home. I got up every so often to add this or that to my sack. I remembered I must take the first confessions of love from the secret drawer in my desk. What about the ring from the fair which a parrot had plucked out for me, for good luck? I will put it on my finger. It's not gold, surely they will let

65

me keep it. And who will be scratching around in my box of secrets tomorrow?

In my half-sleep I saw that my father, mother and I were getting ready for an unknown, dangerous place, full of ice, snow and howling wolves. Are we well enough prepared for such danger I wondered? We mustn't forget anything – a scout's knife, matches, string ... When the doors are closed behind us tomorrow, we can't return even for a needle, or for Father's glasses or a forgotten sock; in brief, for *anything*.

I may have slept for a while, for the last time in my bed, in the safety of my home.

The final days and hours before leaving home for the detention camp had been made worse for me because Grandfather was with us. He had become a different man. I had never ever seen nor could ever have imagined him to be so full of sadness and despair. In 1915, when he married my widowed grandmother, I think he aimed to protect all the members of her family and create a pleasant life for them. And now this man, strong, clever and just, could do nothing. He had tried to use his Aryan status to adopt me. He thought, at least, that he could extricate me from the ruthlessly anti-Jewish Nuremberg Laws. Officially, the adoption was carried out, and even after the war my name was Jana Renée Siegrová-Friesová. But in 1942 adoption did not help. 'Origin' was counted back to goodness knows which generation. Adoption carried no weight against the bureaucratically administered plan of the Nazis to eradicate the Jews, the plan concealed under the heading 'the final solution to the Jewish question'.

Grandfather had arrived from Mnichovo Hradiště and Grandma had stayed at home, probably feeling even more bereft than usual. She knew that we were packing up and what she felt is hard to imagine. Grandpa sat huddled and silent in the corner of the room. Neither my attempts, nor the efforts of my parents, could enliven him. He just did not react. He had completely lost his lifelong belief in goodness, truth and humanity. He feared for us, he feared for his beloved wife. He was aware of his powerlessness.

The next day, all the occupants of our apartment walked out onto the landing in the chilly early morning. Father locked up for the last time, locking our home with keys which were no longer ours. The ornate copper nameplate remained on the door.

In the early winter's morning the streets were deserted. We piled our things onto the waiting carts and began the trek to Jaroměř station, about three kilometres away. My grandfather was the only person who accompanied us on this walk.

The passenger train takes about half an hour between Jaroměř and Hradec Králové, as they are only a few kilometres apart. In spite of that, as I sat on Grandpa's lap with my head buried in his greatcoat, that half-hour seemed much longer, perhaps because my head was drenched with his tears. I cried as well, especially when I thought of my absent grandmother. But probably I was not feeling as wretched as Grandfather. I was fifteen years old and the experience of being locked up for so many months in the claustrophobic atmosphere of our ghetto-like apartment had aroused in me a longing for activity and change. Even in our wildest flights of imagination, the adults, let alone I, could not envisage the experiences that were to come.

We were not the only ones with bundles at the station in Hradec Králové. We had left the carts behind and, along with the hundreds of other Jews arriving from sundry towns and villages in the Hradec Králové district, we trudged wearily along the dark streets in the early morning. The college set up as our detention centre was about a quarter of an hour's walk from the station. When the doors of that school were closed behind us, we were finally cut off from the outside world.

Christmas time was probably chosen for our transport because the school would be empty. In every corridor desks which had been brought out of the classrooms were piled up. On the floor in each room mattresses lay close together. But there were not enough for everybody. In some cases, three people had to make do with two mattresses. It did not seem to create much of a nuisance, as sleep was far from everyone's thoughts. How many of us were there in one classroom? I do not know, but we were head to head. It was our first experience of a complete loss of privacy.

During that same day we made our way one after another to tables where SS officers were seated. Registration: name, age, former address. The house keys were handed in. Everyone also had to hand in their valuables – earrings, rings and even watches. Time had ceased to play a part in our lives. Time as a personal and social regulator had in fact lost all meaning. Instead, there was an imposed routine.

After registration, people clustered together in the classrooms and whispered, communicating their anxieties, their assumptions and fears.

Nobody knew anything for certain. Mass insecurity and ignorance were the principles upon which the system was built and by which, quite quietly, millions were being shunted to violent deaths.

I should like to recall something less sombre from those first few days, but nothing of that kind stays in my memory. As yet, no one knew the word 'holocaust', but already it was happening.

The next day, for the first time, I witnessed physical assault against the powerless by those in a position of absolute power. The assault took place in a corridor, unexpectedly and quickly. It was only later that the horror of it gradually dawned on me. We were permitted to move around the corridors, so people looked for their relatives or even acquaintances. A man I did not know, who was wearing a star, turned from the main corridor into a side one. He was looking for the toilet. We were on the first floor, and the toilets on this floor were apparently not for us but for the Germans, the SS. The man wearing the star did not realise that. He was near the toilet when an SS guard emerged from it. Without warning the guard, in his black uniform, hurled himself at the Jewish man and screamed how dare he go anywhere other than where he was allowed. He thumped the man with his fists until the man was knocked to the ground, then he kicked him. Without realising what I was doing, I flung myself in the men's direction. Several pairs of arms grabbed me and pulled me back into the nearest classroom. Hysterically, I jerked about and tried to wrench myself from them. I failed.

When silence filled the corridor someone must have fetched my mother because I found myself in her arms. As if from afar, I heard her soothing voice and her thanks to my rescuers. I did not really understand why she was thanking them. Then, loudly and with relief, I burst into tears. It was not easy to comprehend the immense change in our lives.

We remained in this first prison, the erstwhile school, for three days. For the whole time we could wash ourselves only in the basins in the toilets, and we had to wear ski clothes because the school's heating had been turned off.

On the fourth day, in the early morning chill and darkness, we dragged our bundles back to the Hradec Králové station. Evidently my beloved grandfather had waited those three days so that he could see us once more, even from a distance. He stood on the footpath as we walked in the street – we were forbidden now to walk on the footpath. Grandfather, who had always been tall, was so shrunken with misery that he now seemed tiny. He walked beside us to the station. For the last time, I turned my head to catch a glimpse of him and a thought occurred to me: what would he have done if he had not had to return to Grandmother?

That was the last time I saw him.

It was 23 December 1942. Perhaps the Germans did not want to arouse attention by herding us into cattle wagons in the middle of Bohemia during the Christmas season. Instead, we went to the Terezín ghetto in a passenger train. Our special train stopped often and for long periods of time, and it spent hours on adjacent tracks. Some people lost their first distressing uncertainty, at least on the surface, about whatever, wherever, had been decided for us.

'We are going to Terezín, and really that is not so terrible. After all, it is here, in Bohemia.'

Here and there, some people were even cracking war jokes which we already knew, but in order not to disappoint the joke-tellers we responded to them with subdued laughter. There was considerable discussion about why people had not emigrated. After all, a few years ago, so and so's cousin or acquaintance had written from Germany about the plight of the Jews and about concentration camps. Why was it that the disinclination to believe was stronger than common sense? Perhaps because even those who sounded warning bells immediately expressed doubts. 'It is simply not possible. After all, we live in civilised Europe. Germany has produced such great figures as Goethe, Schiller, Heine ...' Finally, if these things were to happen, other countries such as England, America and France would surely intervene?

I listened to the adults' discussions half-heartedly. The other children in our carriage and I eagerly looked out of the windows at the unknown countryside. Smoke rose from chimneys of the houses and we tried to catch sight of people behind their curtained windows. We passed through Prague and the sight of Hradčany Castle was so exciting that I had goose bumps. Perhaps it was also because the winter chill seeped through my warm coat in the unheated carriage.

In spite of our train being stationary more often than not, we finally approached our unfamiliar destination. Gradually people quietened down and became absorbed in their own thoughts. The train jerked and stopped. We realised that we had actually arrived at our train's destination, Bohušovice. At that time, the railway line did not yet go all the way to Terezín. It was dark and only searchlights pierced the darkness. Shouts, orders, flew about – *schnell, schnell!* – and dogs barked.

This was not a nightmare. This was ugly reality.

Floodgate to the ghetto

U ntil December 1942, I had not the faintest knowledge of ghetto conditions. Now about 60,000 people were packed into Terezín. Even in the war years, pre-Christmas days had been full of poetry and goodwill. Now, from one day to the next, this was replaced with anxiety about the unknown, and disgust with filth and the total loss of privacy.

The first step: Bohušovice station platform. The SS, dogs, searchlights in the darkening evening. Shouting. Hundreds of men, women and children somehow hung onto their bundles and cases and lined up for the march from Bohušovice to Terezín. Confused and frightened, we suddenly heard a muffled call. 'Fries family, is the family Fries from Josefov here?'

We turned towards the sound of the voice. It belonged to a tall young man wearing a quilted work jacket. My parents knew him. It was Milan, the twenty-five-year-old son of a wealthy family from Jaroměř. At that moment he seemed to us like an angel from heaven. In a flash he joined this strange, sad procession and, without any explanation, gave us orders: 'Put all your belongings aside and move on. I will look after your baggage. You will get everything back after you have gone through the entry procedures into the ghetto. Nothing will be lost, don't worry.'

It was a miracle. How glad we were to get rid of those burdensome kilograms. How gladly we gave way to the feeling that we were not altogether nameless, that someone knew about us, someone had looked after us.

In the damp darkness, we dragged ourselves into an even darker town. We went through the town gates and along the streets to the barracks which was the destination of all new transports. Worn out, shivering and hunched up with cold, we found ourselves in a badly lit room. There were tables all around, the SS behind them rummaging through people's belongings and confiscating whatever they liked. But our guardian angel appeared – how did he find us? He turned to Father, Mother and me and whispered, 'Come with me.' We made our way through the crowd after him.

'Here is all your baggage, nothing is missing, nobody went through it. Take it and go up there to the first floor. I cannot come with you. When it's possible, I will find you. I still have a few people to help.' He disappeared.

Even now, I can recall the dreamy state of those first few hours that night and the following day. It was as if it did not concern me – it could not be me, or my elegant mother or my kind father walking up a slippery ramp into a huge space, which was probably a stable. Occasionally we tripped across wooden ridges which divided up the ramp. These ridges were helpful. They prevented us from slipping under the weight of our bags. There was a dirty, yellow-brown liquid trickling beneath our feet. It was only later that we realised what had been flowing under us, and had frozen here and there. Urine, human excrement from people who were too weak and sick to get up from their straw mattresses and go to the latrines in the middle of the barracks courtyard.

Our 'angel' was gone. He disappeared as quickly and unobtrusively as he had appeared. He would locate us again but only after several weeks. Right now we almost collapsed under the weight of our bags and Father and I tried to lighten Mother's load. Finally, at the top of the ramp we entered a vast, endless area. There was no room to move. All around, people were lying down or sitting among their bags and suitcases. The day before our arrival, a transport had come from Mladá Boleslav and had not as yet been processed. Into this chaos hundreds and hundreds of others had arrived. No space was made for us, nor for those who had accompanied us, and no one was prepared to share their mattress. We were looked upon as intruders by those who had arrived earlier, though at the same time they were actually glad to see us. As 'established residents' they already knew that one or other of the transports would have to go east.

Someone said, 'Don't make yourselves too comfortable, you are probably moving on. We have been here for a while, we haven't unpacked, why would they send us?' Mladá Boleslavians used a kind of logical argument where logic did not exist.

Only a few naked globes lit up that whole space. From among those in our transport a few of us remained standing. The others eventually found a spot to lodge themselves, surrounded by a herd of 'permanent' inhabitants. In spite of their arriving only a few hours ahead of us, they eagerly asked for the news from the front. They were glad that the Russians were advancing and that the war would end soon. Even after that, nobody moved an inch, and we stood and stood until I felt my legs almost give way.

Again a guardian angel was looking over us and nudged someone whom we knew from the distant past, well before the war years. He took pity on us and suggested we sit next to him on his mattress. What a relief to sit down on the bare mattress, our bags around us. Were we saying to ourselves that this could not last very long, that it made no sense to confine us here unproductively? Perhaps it also occurred to us to wonder how long we could last in this unventilated but icy room. I can remember how I worried about where and how I would change my clothes and wash for the night. How trivial! Gradually, people separated into different groups and the talking went on and on ... speculation, complaints and even astonishment about what was happening.

I have no idea how we survived that first night. The next day, a trickle of people from the ghetto came to see us: acquaintances, relatives and even strangers. Some had been here for ages – well, a month, half a year, some even for a year. After the first greetings and embraces, we, the new ones, could feel some animosity from the ghetto dwellers. It took a while before we realised this. Why, even my Aunt Olga, my grandmother's sister who always loved me and I her, was different somehow. She was strange. Slowly, and in a roundabout way, barely perceptible accusations emerged: how well-off we apparently were; we had had weeks, even months, longer of sleeping in our own beds; how well we looked, we probably lacked nothing; we had brought food supplies; and we were wearing good quality, intact clothes. They had already eaten their supplies, unlike us ... We felt embarrassed in front of them. I can vividly recall that feeling of embarrassment. A greying, unsightly old woman with thin hair, whom no one knew, loudly reproached us, insisting that the arrival of a new transport meant that the previous ones would go east. There was no one else to whom they could shout, whisper or otherwise express the anxiety and fear which had overcome them.

Some time towards morning I had to get up from the mattress, that puny bit of security, and look for a place where I could carry out a primitive human need. The old and the sick could not manage that, and hence the sludge that had trickled under our feet when we arrived. I had to look for a different solution. I found out that the latrines were in the courtyard. The courtyard was large, square and very clean. The building in which we were interned seemed to be part of the barracks complex, and occasionally people appeared in its 'welcoming' portico. I saw the latrine immediately. It was in the middle of this tidy courtyard – a rectangular trench with roughly nailed planks above it. No walls, no doors. Several people could sit there at any one time. The courtyard appeared deserted but recent experiences had not changed me to such an extent that I could cope with the possibility of somebody watching me during this private function. I panicked. What now? I could not tolerate this, it was beyond belief. I had to solve this situation now, without delay. I told myself that I would try to sneak into the forbidden buildings which housed the elderly ghetto residents. People lived there who had surely endured the same horrors as we had. Up a few steps, on the first floor, was a sign: *Eintritt Verboten* – Entry Forbidden. Past the sign were the sought-after doors. How grateful I was. I realised that a person does not have to abide by every order. Probably those older than I would not risk anything, would not look for an alternative; they would rather rather suffer the humiliation of the latrine in the courtyard.

Quietly, I opened the door and I was overwhelmed by the damp and the smell of disinfectant. How pleasant. I hurried, but noticed that an old lady, all skin and bone although neatly dressed in black, was sitting at the rear of quite a large room. I hid my number CH 18 under my jumper. In spite of this, my plump cheeks and good clothing made

74

her realise that I was a newcomer. She screamed piercingly at me. Even though I did not understand her German (much later on, I began to distinguish the Berlin from the Viennese accent), I well understood her tone and gestures. She wanted to throw me out. In my poor German, I explained and I flattered her – how clean she kept the toilet, using disinfectant, and what it meant to me not to have to go to the latrine. The old woman came and stood in front of the toilet door and indicated quite clearly to me that if I did not leave, she would make a scene. And she, a Jewess, threw me, also a Jewess and similarly afflicted, out. Still in a state of shock, I slinked over to the latrine in the middle of the courtyard. No one was about. Lucky me.

I do not remember if two or three days passed before they moved us from the 'floodgate'. My parents went to look for acquaintances and relatives whose ghetto addresses we knew before we left home, when we had sent them the permitted half-kilogram parcels. Father and Mother wanted to find someone who could advise us how to procure our own mattresses in the barracks or houses to give us a base, a feeling of identity and also an address to which my grandfather and grandmother could write.

In that December, the ghetto was bursting at its seams. Every day, other transports arrived from various districts in Bohemia and Moravia. Nobody worried about housing people. The Germans did not care how the Jewish Council tackled this insoluble problem. The Council was almost powerless. Bewildered, cold and sad after the experience of the floodgate, we wandered about the ghetto and looked for help. My parents and I had worked out some meeting points if we found accommodation. If this failed, Father had decided to seek out his brother Josef whom he knew was the *Hausälteste*, administrator, in one of the houses.

Before we found this uncle, I roamed around the streets aimlessly. The narrow, straight streets of the former Terezín fortress were unbelievably overcrowded. Was everyone hurrying somewhere? While still at home, I used to have nightmares from which I awoke terrified, but no nightmare was as terrible as this reality. I wonder why I was not overpowered by fear, but rather by curiosity? What would come next, what could happen to me? It even occurred to me that perhaps it would be the re-emergence of our guardian angel, the young man who had led us through our first predicament here.

More significantly, that day, I saw a cart pulled by human beings. I pushed my way through the throng. I saw a two-wheeled cart on which was a messy heap of things resembling bodies. Unfortunately I did not believe my first impression, and without thinking what I was doing I stepped closer. Yes, they were bodies, stiff and unreal, thrown here and there, legs and arms dangling from the cart. The cart-pullers occasionally stopped to straighten up the load. When I realised that I was not mistaken, I became rigid. I could not move. People bumped into me. Until that moment I had never seen a corpse. And now this.

The anguished realisation that a human being can have so little worth was the revelation of my first day in the ghetto. Later, nothing, or almost nothing, was as horrifying.

In the ghetto, people were unable to receive their regular ration of food if they were not registered for work. The weekly ration consisted of a 50-gram bag of sugar, 50 grams of margarine and a quarter loaf of bread, and it was an incentive to people to find work. Mother found work for me in the wooden workshops run by Mr Hermann, where work clothes and other goods were sewn on old machines. It was all right.

I had known Mr Hermann since I was five years old. Until recently, he had his own elegant fabrics shop in the main square in Mladá Boleslav, a half-hour bus ride from Mnichovo Hradiště. Although I went there often with Grandmother, it was always a real outing. I loved the chocolate biscuits filled with candied fruit and nuts, and the freshly roasted chestnuts bought from an old woman in front of the church in winter. Mladá Boleslav was almost a big city for me and when my grandmother decided to take me there every week for ballet lessons I was thrilled. Ballet classes were in the ballroom of the imposing Grand Hotel. While I was bruising my toes trying to do pirouettes in pink satin ballet shoes, Grandmother was drinking coffee in the lounge. Once the class had finished, I joined her there and, without exception, had an ice-cream sundae. That was wonderful, but still not the most· exciting part of the experience.

'Armless Frantík', a neatly dressed man, used to sit at another table. He really was lacking arms but, despite that, held a newspaper on the marble-topped table, using his feet. He wore no socks, but his feet were clean and as he simply seemed part of the coffee-lounge, no one showed any surprise. I was forbidden to stare at him. I thought up various pretexts so that I could pass by his table as closely as possible. He held the newspaper between his toes and with no shilly-shallying turned the pages. With the same dexterity he would hold a cup of coffee, stir sugar in it and, without spilling a drop, bring the cup to his lips.

Before going home, Grandmother often popped into Mr Hermann's spacious shop next to the hotel. I loved going there. The shop had long, polished, wooden counters and, behind them, shelves full of beautiful fabrics. Everything suggested quality, and Mr Hermann himself, a tall, slim man, looked more like Gary Cooper than the owner of a textile business. I really liked him. He always greeted us with a smile. He usually gave me a little bundle of samples – wool and silk, plain and multicoloured. The pile of squares was lovely and with them I sewed little skirts, blouses, dresses and pyjamas for my dolls. Sometimes we climbed up the metal spiral staircase at the back of the shop, which led into his office, and he offered me a sweet and Grandmother a liqueur. Mr Hermann had a beautiful twenty-year-old daughter, Helena. At that time I knew nothing more about him or his family.

Suddenly, he was here, in Terezín. I do not know how Mother found him. He was still tall and handsome, but thinner. He was the supervisor of the numerous workshops employing women in Terezín. They sewed in the winter for about eleven hours a day in a poor light. I did not really know how to sew, but Mr Hermann, who had not forgotten our pre-war friendship, found work for me which was convenient and comfortable. He led me to a room where three quiet girls were sitting. They hardly answered my greeting, only whispered their names. There was a tangle of indistinguishable things on the floor in front of them. Each girl had her own pile. The rest of the room was filled with coloured bundles piled one on top of the other.

Mr Hermann left me with the girls and the bundles. Irma tossed the first bundle onto the floor in front of me. I undid it and its contents spilled out everywhere. There was an unbelievable assortment of things – the contents of drawers from dressing-tables, dressers and kitchen tables, the most ordinary yet most intimate odds and ends in the world. I really do not know how the things came to be in the bundles. I can only surmise that, after the Jewish people had been deported from their homes, squads of SS haphazardly emptied all the drawers into sheets, large towels and tablecloths. These bundles, tied by their corners, were deposited at Mr Hermann's workshop. Our task was simple:

77

untie the bundles and sort everything out. One bundle a day was the norm. The work was some of the lightest and did not need much effort. The hardest thing was to understand how the tangled heaps had originated.

I panicked right from the start. Silk cottons and coarse threads, thimbles, measuring tapes, pins and needles and even scissors had to be sorted out. Loose cotton had to be wound onto spools and put to one side. Everything had a use in the workshops. That was only part of the task. Many other things had to be sorted: albums and individual photographs of whole generations; pairs of glasses, some with only one lens, some with no lenses at all, manicure sets, nail scissors and files; an envelope with 'Ruth' written on it in red ink and, inside, a lock of golden hair; pince-nez, false teeth, pin cushions, pipes, dolls and teddy bears chewed by the toothless gums of babies, years ago; cutlery and, here and there, a serviette with an imprint of gravied lips on it. And many, many letters in Czech and German, dating from the beginning of the century or from only a few years before.

I waited in fear that I would pick up a photograph and see a known, dear face. So many of those women in the yellowed photographs resembled my grandmother of years ago when, in a long, wasp-waisted dress, she leaned on a lace parasol, and posed with an artificial palm tree in the background. Grandfather, in his striped trousers and white jacket, a straw hat on his head, sat by her feet.

Where are these girls in their high lace-up boots, and the boys in their sailor suits leaning on penny-farthing bicycles, so much bigger than they, which they raced across the fields fifty years ago? Who got permission to throw them on this heap like useless rubbish?

This job was only a seemingly comfortable beginning to slavery. Mr Hermann occasionally peeped through the door, smiled apologetically at me, and disappeared. I worked there for about a week. By then, I found my way around better, and had obtained work by myself – harder but more bearable. I carried worn-out shoes in bags from the barracks to the shoemaker's workshop and, once repaired, back again. At that time the most important thing for me was to believe that perhaps the shoes belonged to living people.

After some weeks – it's difficult to remember how many – through the help of a kind friend, I was given a bunk in the *Mädchenheim* (Girls' Home). Girls from there, up to the age of fourteen, worked in the gardens, and we older ones worked in the fields around Terezín.

How lucky we were to leave the ghetto in a work gang every day for the country and, on the horizon, see a hill behind Litoměřice, and to sometimes work near the Ohře river! It was hard work, but no matter how hard it was, anything was better than untying fateful bundles filled with sadness.

But before the onset of the relatively good time among the girls in the *Mädchenheim*, I was to experience a nasty time in Q Street.

The house in Q Street

Despite his being in Terezín, Uncle Josef's cheeks were rosy pink and chubby. He was about sixty, and had a clear complexion even though he lived behind the ramparts of that ghetto-town. His face could not provoke anyone because he rarely left his house. The house on Q Street was, in a sense, his house, as he was the *Hausältester*, the ruler. This position brought with it a precious privilege: a room of his own, two by two metres, with a door closing him off from the outside world. Inside, there was a bed, a small stove, a sink, a table and chair. All of this was shared with his wife, my Aunt Frances. The unpleasant side of Uncle's privileged position was his responsibility for implementing orders, for the smooth and, if possible, inconspicuous running of the house. He was troubled by the knowledge of what would happen if anything occurred which, according to the rules in force, might be described as incorrect. In a way, Uncle knew how to handle things and the advantages of that house were worth a little uncertainty.

At first glance, the building was repellent because of its ugliness and neglected state. But from a resident's point of view, that was a good thing – the peeling stucco, walls damp up to the first floor, chipped-off corners and missing window panes. Beyond a dirty, smelly passage one saw a yard full of useless rubbish – an oval, sightless dressing-table mirror, an old hat-stand, rusty pipes, a gutted damp straw mattress, the remains of a four-wheel cart, and so on. In brief, death and decay emanated so strongly from those walls that the inspection parties were afraid to cross the threshold. Who was to know, there might be typhoid, or infectious hepatitis, or encephalitis? Better give the place a wide berth. And what more could Uncle Josef wish for? In his house there was calm, tranquillity, no movement – and this in a town of constant movement with transports arriving and departing.

The house was full to bursting point, as indeed was nearly every corner in Terezín in 1942. It was crammed full of people who, even by local standards, were unusual. Transports would arrive from the German Reich with old people, very old Jews from the Reich. They believed that they were being moved from their homes to the Terezín Spa. Of course, they were confused. As far as their strength allowed after a train journey of many days' duration, they demanded to be treated with respect. They behaved with dignity, conscious of their legitimate demands. There were carefully turned-out old ladies, with nets on their sparse hair, and severe *Hofräte* (councillors) in tight, pin-striped trousers in which they hoped, one day, to be laid to rest in respectable family tombs. Surely, the fact that they had been transported like cattle was simply due to the war? But now that they had arrived in Terezín, they would insist on their rights, such as accommodation in a hotel with proper meals. Had not the Berlin Jewish community contributed a million marks to their transportation? They knew the worth of money. They knew the value of promises which the German authorities had given them in Berlin. That their luggage had not yet arrived was probably due to some mistake. They were convinced that the jewellery and money that they had handed over at home would be deposited in the local bank. After all, they held receipts. Until quite recently, these beliefs had some meaning. Their reasoning was in terms of known morality and legality, which they had been taught by their forefathers and by the order-loving Germans.

The arrival of any new transport was always difficult for Uncle Josef. He could not refuse to inspect, at least cursorily, all those documents regarding the transfer of property, land, factories or houses, all witnessed by public notaries and endorsed with decorative rubber stamps. He had to listen to the recital of laws, decrees and promises. There was no point in trying to tell them about the total collapse of legal and moral standards. He had tried to do so at first, but no one had believed him. So he just listened patiently; there was nothing else he could do. To find lifelong concepts of legality, truth, honour, good and evil tottering, in one's old age, was hard. Many a sharp word and insult rained down on his head, the head of a bad mediator between the newly-arrived and the state. To them he was a bad administrator and servant. But he could take that for a day or two. He knew what would happen. The luggage would not arrive. They had nothing beyond the clothes they stood up in. They were each assigned a dirty mattress (one that had been used again and again) and given access to cold water, provided the frost had not burst the pipes. While they still had some strength they would spend hours in the freezing streets, queuing for tepid black liquid in the morning and for green bean soup at midday, sometimes with potatoes, sometimes with turnip-leaf cabbage. Uncle's 'tenants' rapidly weakened. Their worn overcoats, which became dirtier and dirtier, didn't provide much warmth. The ration for non-workers was not enough to keep them alive: a quarter loaf of bread, ten grams of sugar and ten grams of margarine. At night, lice, bed-bugs and fleas, small but cruel enemies, drained the last remnants of their strength.

The tenants soon stopped shaking their little fists, soon stopped shouting and quarrelling. They lay one on top of the other, crammed into what used to be furnished rooms in a provincial house in Terezín but which now contained nothing except straw mattresses and human beings. Only a few days earlier they had not known one another. Now they were breathing, excreting and dying next to each other, almost as closely as in an embrace. The bustle of the first few days after the arrival of a new transport calmed down and the sounds became weaker.

We knew of nowhere else we could go to in this ancient fortress town. Empress Maria Theresa had had it built according to the rules of eighteenth-century military geometry: the outer band a defensive ditch, the second, the fortifications, and the third, the barracks. Within were straight streets with houses of equal height for the civilians. A year before, the town had held between six and seven thousand people including the troops. Now, almost 60,000 Jews were pressed into that same space. In that situation, the ghetto's administration could think of no other solution than that of letting the newcomers find 'their' mattresses and 'their' bunks, mostly without any organised assistance.

Uncle Josef was our only hope. With the warmth of our abandoned home in the pockets of our overcoats, we found ourselves terrified and helpless, standing in front of Uncle in his little room, still with the numbers CH 16, CH 17 and CH 18 on strings around our necks.

Father's brother Josef was the only one of his nine siblings whose whereabouts we knew. Only a few days earlier we had been sending him the permitted 500-gram food packets from 'outside'. He received us with obvious discomfort. His anxiety that our arrival might drag him into some new, unfamiliar situation was obvious. What do you want from me? his eyes seemed to be saying. You had quite a few months more in your home than I had, so do not upset my painstakingly won peace. I want to sit quietly within my four walls. I do not know what is going on, either in the ghetto or beyond the ramparts. Your arrival has created an upheaval in my oasis, and because of my heart problem I am not supposed to get excited. Anyway, he could not do anything for us, not a thing. It was not in his power to find us a corner in which to settle down. Maybe we were misled by his being a *Hausältester*. It meant absolutely nothing, except a dangerous responsibility for him, that was certain! And even if he could find some extra space in his house, he would not be able to sleep easily at the thought that his brother and family were here among these lice-infested, dirty, dying wrecks. Nor could he help us in any other way, he hurriedly added. His wife, Aunt Frances, worked in the *Wärmeküche* (community kitchen) but that meant no more than that. Now and again she might bring home an extra morsel of food, a log of firewood, or a few lumps of coal. Even if we had food to heat we couldn't count on it, because coal was like gold here, yes, like gold ...

He talked and talked. The monotonous flow of his words, more than anything else, convinced us that what had happened was not just a bad dream, from which we might wake at any moment. Home was irretrievably vanishing in the distance. The sounds coming from Uncle's lips took on meanings that none of us had known before. Besides, he almost whispered, he was not allowed to take in anyone under sixty, this was a house for the aged.

Silence fell. Then Uncle's voice disturbed that soundless pause: 'You'll find out for yourselves what I mean,' and we realised that he did not have the strength to turn us out into the unlit, piercingly cold, Terezín street.

'What can I do, what can I do? All right, stay here. But not a word about our blonde daughter Lily. I don't want to hear about her or about her brother. They were old enough to answer for their actions. All

83

right, they didn't get on the train with us, so now they are dependent on the goodwill and the courage of strangers. Of their own free will they exchanged the evil certainty – but at least a certainty – of being deported with us for uncertainty and a temporary hiding place. How can anyone hope to evade that relentless Nazi machine? Suppose they get caught? What will happen to them then? And what will happen to us? No, don't tell me, I don't want to know ...'

Guilty and ashamed, the three of us stood in front of that stranger. Not so long ago, he had successfully and proudly managed his stationery shop in the Královské Vinohrady district of Prague. I had never been to their home. Our families did not get on. Lily and her brother Eda had occasionally come to see us in the country during holidays, for a change from 'unhealthy' Prague. Children, as a rule, know little about family relationships, but I had an idea that 'Uncle Josef is a good man, but that unpleasant Frances ...' Perhaps, this was due partly to the different lifestyles of my mother and her sister-in-law. Aunt Frances would stand behind the counter of her husband's stationery shop from morning to night, while my mother 'enjoyed herself on one Riviera after another, driving about in a car, wrapped in furs and the fragrance of French perfume,' as my aunt later told me reproachfully more than once.

Now, pressed skin-to-skin in that tiny little room, we were facing a breathless man who was convincing himself, and us, that he was right in not wishing to have his present world destroyed. I don't know how my parents felt, but I felt ashamed. My uncle had been here for several months and that meant an eternity. Whereas we, a mere three days ago, had still slept in our own beds, albeit in a flat now shared by three Jewish families. We had eaten at our dining table, off porcelain plates, and had bathed in our bathroom. Was it possible that only three days ago I had played the piano, and when I raised my head, had seen branches blooming with snow in our garden? True, even at the collection point we had heard comments such as 'What do you newcomers really know?' And had our life been all that easy? Were not those days and nights after the assassination of Heydrich days of anxiety and sleeplessness, as we wondered which of our dear ones would be on the list of those executed the following morning? We, too, had been prisoners – not allowed outside the bounds of our native town, not allowed to use public transport, not allowed to meet anyone, not allowed to keep domestic animals, and only permitted to buy our meagre rations during prescribed hours.

In self-defence, I thought fleetingly of how I had suffered from not being allowed to go to school, or to ballet class, how I had suffered when my last girl friend began to make excuses ... No, that was no adequate defence. Anything that happened so far had been comfortable steps in a descent to somewhere that had no comparison with anything previously experienced. How ridiculous was my recent anguish at not being allowed to buy a one-crown standing-room ticket to the cinema, among all those scuffling boys and girls.

Who could explain to me how it was possible that three days ago we locked our humanity behind our front door and handed over the keys? That we locked up an untidy sewing basket, albums with the yellowing photographs of great-grandmothers and great-aunts, the wet pen with which I had written the last entry in my diary, and the intimate smells of our kitchen?

But it had happened. Now we were here, disturbing the regular flow of Uncle Josef's days. Bitter anger rose up within me with the realisation of the finality with which our past had been severed from us. This man standing before us, and we before him, had all become different people. We were acting differently, we were using familiar words with unfamiliar meanings, we looked at things differently. It had happened, we were now in the concentration camp about which we had only spoken in whispers a few days ago. Then and many times afterwards there would be situations when it seemed that the world would come to an end, that we, and everything else, would also come to an end because things just could not go on. But they did go on. They always went on a little way beyond what, a moment earlier, had seemed unimaginable. Life does not give up so easily.

Straw mattresses were found for us, still warm, in the corner of a room on the first floor. Somebody helped us build a wall around it with our suitcases. Somebody helped to hammer a nail into the wall and to stretch a sheet across the corner. Separation from the other bodies on the floor was purely symbolic. The thin material allowed every breath, moan and smell to come through. That night, all three of us, Father, Mother and I, witnessed the gates of death open three times, so that we would look at the three empty mattresses with new eyes in the morning. Uncle had not been mistaken. That morning we were determined to go anywhere rather than stay there.

But miracles sometimes happen. All night, apparently, my uncle and aunt had discussed what to do with us, and had come up with a solution. The house had a large empty attic. He pointed out how unusual such an empty space was in Terezín, where every metre was used vertically and horizontally. The reason was that the official commission had written it off: it could not be heated, it lacked the most basic facilities and the windows were broken. But if we wished, he would break the rules for our sake until we found a better place.

Everything is relative. After last night, this was a way out and we accepted it gratefully. I believe that once I conjured up a piece of home in the most convenient corner of the attic, I actually felt happy. My parents went off to find some friends, some help, those threads that were necessary for life. When I had made sleeping places for the three of us, using every warm thing we had brought, and had put a book on a rafter by my side, with a notebook, a pencil and my grey felt monkey, I regained a sense of security and territorial ownership. I knew that things were more difficult for my parents, more difficult because of their adult ability to foresee what was for me unforeseeable.

Life as a family in the attic, that dark December, was not of long duration. Father, God knows how, or with whose help, got a good job with the gang of carpenters who, frequently, even worked outside the ramparts. He was given his first bunk in the Hanover Barracks which were assigned to men who were able to work. As for Mother, a doctor cousin took her into the TB department as a patient, among the seriously ill, even though she was as sound as a bell, because it was believed during those months that tubercular patients were not being deported to the east. So I remained in the attic on my own.

At that time the solitude of my attic was welcome. The door could be bolted from inside. This very facility of being able to lock yourself in, in a prison town, enhanced the sense of uniqueness and luxury. What was more, since I was not on any lists, I did not exist. The frost chilled me to the bone and often I would wake up with a dusting of snow on the quilted eiderdown we had brought with us. Where my breath reached, there was even a thin covering of ice. In these arctic conditions, I felt content, wearing all my sweaters, skiing socks and a track suit, buried like a mole, with only my eyes, nose and one hand outside. The attic window let through just enough light for me to read the books I had smuggled into our luggage. They were *Thorn Roof* by Younghill Kang, an inspiring account of people trying to survive under Japanese occupation in Korea, and poetry. I was soon to realise how important it had been for me to exchange some food for the body for food for the mind, within the permitted allowance of 50 kilograms per head. Later, I was to discover that hundreds and thousands of others had reasoned likewise, so volumes of poetry, art history, the history of mankind, novels, opera scores and musical literature all turned up in Terezín. Everyone chose what, at that moment, was closest to his or her heart, and the cases under the bunks in the concentration camp were real treasure chests. Of course, it was forbidden. Even the Germans knew what powers of resistance resided in art. These treasures were passed on by those who were deported further east, because all they were permitted was a rucksack, and even that proved superfluous.

My world was then the world of two Czech writers – Jiří Wolker, Fráňa Šrámek – and French poetry. Onto the beam above my head, where a splinter had peeled off, I pinned Jiří Wolker's little poem 'At the Palmist's':

> This short line here means a short span of life
> and your hand, sir, is marked by a short line.
> The gods have granted you but a short life
> and soon you'll die.

But close to this funereal poem hung another, one I had known by heart since I was twelve – the middle stanzas of Kipling's 'If':

> If you can dream – and not make dreams your master;
> If you can think – and not make thoughts your aim:
> If you can meet with Triumph and Disaster
> And treat those two impostors just the same;
> If you can bear to hear the truth you've spoken
> Twisted by knaves to make a trap for fools,
> Or watch the things you gave your life to broken,
> And stoop and build 'em up with worn-out tools.
>
> If you can make one heap of all your winnings
> And risk it on one turn of pitch-and-toss,
> And lose, and start again at your beginnings
> And never breathe a word about your loss;
> If you can force your heart and nerve and sinew
> To serve your turn long after they are gone,
> And so hold on when there is nothing in you
> Except the Will which says to them: 'Hold on!'

At that time, Wolker and Kipling spoke straight to my heart. At the age of fifteen, it does not take long to find reasons for living, just as to find reasons against. My attic seemed to favour the will to live. The transition from night to day and from day to night was almost imperceptible in that snowy twilight. No one bothered about me, and I was slowly consuming the high-value food we had brought with us: ship's biscuits, chocolate caramels, meat baked into bread. Only a few sounds drifted up from below. From a fear of exhausting my reading matter too quickly, I attempted to write. Love poems full of not-yet-lived experiences appeared on my scraps of paper. I rolled these papers up into thin cylinders, pushed them between the beams and dreamed that, long after my death, someone would discover them, and how significant this would be for mankind.

Now and again, though rarely, someone would knock and I would enjoy the thought that I might open up but need not. After some brief hesitation, I invariably did. Sometimes it was my aunt or uncle, but mostly it was Frau Jastrow. She was one of those who had come from the Reich. It was she who had helped us that first night to settle into that unforgettable room below. I was as scared as a rabbit then and was unaware of her presence. Now she would come, drift about the room, beg for something to eat from my case and vanish again.

Frau Jastrow was incredibly, almost fascinatingly, ugly. She belonged to the house more than anything else did. Her back was bent at a right angle. Greasy strands of grey hair hung around a face that was shrivelled like an old apple. Her long bony arms virtually touched the floor. Her nails were like those of the old hag who set up the fatal spinning wheel for Sleeping Beauty. As for her eyes, you could never see them. They were directed to the ground. Those sleeping on the floor below, in the rooms I was trying to forget, probably knew her eyes well. It was she who was their link with the world. She would collect their verbal, and sometimes even written, complaints but would never pass them on. For these slight services, she would accept their last family brooches, smuggled in the lining of their clothes. Into her thin, twisted fingers slipped the last gold wedding rings that were testaments to old loves or parental arrangements.

For Uncle Josef, Frau Jastrow was the most important person in the house. In fact, she was indispensable. He himself hardly ever went out into the street, which was a place of dangerous infection and other pitfalls. As I have said before, he locked himself up in his retreat and did not want to know what was happening outside his door. Only rarely was he in direct contact with the tenants in his house. All data about changes in the house, which he entered on questionnaires and report forms, was collected by Frau Jastrow. The administrative work connected with the operation of such a house was considerable and Uncle was always kept busy. To enable the smooth running of the machine which liquidated millions of people, lots of precise data was necessary. Like the rest of them, Uncle did not know the purpose for which he was working so painstakingly. Frau Jastrow swished through the house here and there, effortlessly descending the spiral staircase and effortlessly ascending it. This dilapidated house had accepted her and included her in its inventory. Her desiccated little body and the decaying house contrasted with her joyful, provocative vitality. God knows where she derived such energy from.

Uncle would receive her every morning. Apart from her, no stranger was allowed into his lair. Once, by sheer chance, I was present during her morning report on changes during the night. There was no indifference in her voice, but neither was there sadness. There was something more like excitement and, it seemed to me, satisfaction – as if she were assessing her own chances of survival by the departure of others. I recalled the energetic eagerness with which she had bedded us down among those awaiting death that first night. Again and again I had seen her in the mornings, while it was still dark, preparing the stretchers with the dead for the orderlies who would carry them away. For that reason alone I was terribly scared of her. If I had to be near her, I took great care not to touch her, not even with a sleeve. I was ashamed of being so afraid of her and I hoped she would not notice. I did not want her to know that I knew it was she who helped herself to more of my supplies than I offered; that I knew who scavenged under the pillows of the dying on the floor below, taking what was not given to her. Unwittingly, I fawned on her and I could not bear the sense of humiliation I felt about it. My resolution to behave differently towards her invariably came to nothing. She was amoral. Anything she wanted she took for herself and she did not care what I thought about her. That was the kind of house it was, and that was the kind of person Frau Jastrow was.

My aunt left for the *Wärmeküche* early in the morning and returned late. Even so, it was considered an exceptionally good job. In a room with two stoves, fired modestly but at least fired, the inhabitants of the ghetto could warm up or cook food from their own supplies – from the 500-gram packets they were permitted to have sent to them. Two women 'cooks', who did not cook, supervised, watching that no more fuel was burnt than the coal ration, and generally ensuring order. For this supervision they were rewarded with small amounts of food. Some of it they kept, some they gave to the coal carriers because their favour was indispensable. As a 'cook', my aunt would bring home a little food, a few sticks of firewood and some coal. She was the bread-winner and my uncle fully recognised her importance. Aunt was cantankerous and argumentative, with a sharp beak-like nose, certainly no beauty. But she made up for that by self-assurance. In her presence, Uncle did not talk much, but was attentive and polite. How much of it was a desire to be left in peace, and how much the remnants of some former closeness, was impossible to determine. Physically, and per-haps also mentally, he was almost motionless. He conserved his strength to a marked degree. Aunt supported that motionless state. Maybe it suited her domineering nature, or perhaps it was a substitute for her lost children's dependence. She had the pride of a gardener who had succeeded in growing roses in the wrong kind of soil.

My aunt did not like me and I believed I understood why. She would rather have had her own children with her than me. I did not hold it against her. She was afraid for her Lily and Eda, who had elected to escape from the transport to which they had been assigned with their parents. Aunt was convinced that with her, under her protective wings, they would have been much safer. She would sob, 'There's such a lot I could give them here, my dearest ones, and who knows where they are and what they are suffering now?' These were her only moments of tenderness. I avoided her whenever possible.

I soon came to regard the attic as my own and I did not expect anyone or anything else. But then my uncle turned up. He stood on the stairs, shivering with cold. He said he felt uneasy at the thought of me being cold and alone.

'Come down to me, child,' he said softly.

I was surprised to find this unexpected offer moving. Then I real-ised that I was chilled through to the marrow. I gladly accepted and every day, once my aunt had left, I would slip down the cold passage to the little room with the window and with the residual warmth of the night before. A room with a table and a chair, a proper bed with mat-tresses on it and suitcases underneath. On the table a saucepan still stood from last night's supper. Together, all this created a little domesticity, a quiet corner, a safe territory. Uncle sat on the chair, a blanket across his knees, his hands in gloves with their fingers cut off, so that he could write more easily and cross out and calculate. He was forever busy with the facts and figures that concealed so many tragic fates. Crouched in a corner on the bed and remaining very still, I too tried to conserve some warmth.

Frau Jastrow would make her report before my arrival, so the peace was undisturbed. I slowly read my book, word by word, desperately wishing that the remaining pages would not get fewer. Now and again I would lift my head and watch the silent person in front of me. His nose had the same shape as my father's – and as mine. His chin was softer and weaker than Father's – and mine. I asked myself some unanswerable questions. What is he like? Good, wicked, desperate, indifferent, empty? What was hidden behind that mask? When a person keeps silent he can be whatever we want him to be. But I attributed to him noble thoughts and great goals, unaccomplished because fate had been cruel. Uncle had eliminated action from his life. That was why it was so extraordinary that he had climbed up to the attic, overcome his fear of my aunt, and invited me into his warm retreat. We got used to one another, we did not disturb each other, and at least we were not alone.

One day, Uncle came out with a stunning offer: 'You can wash down here, child, it's warmer.'

Those who do not know what washing facilities and lavatories were like in Terezín cannot fully appreciate that offer. This, at first, had been for me the most frightful and least acceptable side of life here. Washing was just about bearable, except for the desperate cold. The only reason I went through my daily routine, fetching the water with a basin borrowed from Frau Jastrow, was that I was terrified of bedbugs and lice, which got a foothold wherever there was dirt. That routine meant climbing down the narrow stairs in the dirty-grey morning, walking along the passage, being careful not to kick the odd stretcher with its silent load and, on the way back with the water, getting hold of the attic door and kicking it shut behind me. Then, taking off sweaters and track suit, I had to overcome my revulsion to icy water. I was helped by willpower and fear. Things were indescribably worse with the lavatory-ditches; willpower was useless there, and I used to cry with revulsion. I cannot bear to say any more about that side of existence in Terezín.

How gratefully I accepted the offer of my grey-haired uncle, with his rose-parchment cheeks and his rounded back. But that was not all. Next day, old Frau Jastrow came to tell me she had lit the range and *heated* some water for me. Aunt would not know the difference, just a few bits of firewood. It was a miracle in that freezing January and I nearly cried from bliss and emotion, the rapture of intimate contact with warm water and of soaping myself with the pink soap bought from the chemist's at the corner of our street at home. The soap slipped from one hand to the other and the lather slid willingly down my skin. I was overcome with gratitude, happiness and warmth which blended with the stuffy atmosphere of the little room. How could I thank my uncle for that precious privacy, for his courage in secretly burning a few logs?

This idyllic state, however, was cut short one day when my presence was discovered and I had to report for work one frosty morning. I was assigned to carry sacks full of repaired boots to the barracks. But a few days later I was inexplicably relieved of that exhausting and depressing job and I returned to my attic. The following morning I washed with even greater relish than before. With one leg in the basin and my body all wet, I turned my head to thank Uncle once more, when my eyes met his. His eyes were not veiled by the mist of indifference behind which he used to hide. At that moment they were wide open, clear, and full of concupiscent madness. He was not an uncle and I was not a child. I became aware of my pubescence, its unattractiveness and its burden. How inconvenient it was, and how hideous!

So that was the good deed. My uncle was hiding behind his papers, motionless and inconspicuous, and I, like a fool, had believed that he had given me this pleasurable comfort out of the goodness of his heart, and for nothing. Just wait, Father is going to kill you, Aunt Frances will not give you anything to eat, I silently threatened. Not a single sound broke the tension while I quickly washed off the repulsively clinging suds with the small amount of cooling water. I suddenly realised how dirty the towel was and I was choking with its stench in the unaired room. I finally forced my stiff fingers to move more swiftly and, at last, the whole process was finished, and my track suit and sweaters restored some sense of security.

Slowly, I mopped up the spattered floor, regretting that I had ever turned my head. How much longer could I now enjoy this place of refuge? Now that I knew, surely I could not ... or maybe I could?

Perhaps I was wrong and nothing had happened, I had not seen anything? He was a poor old man, locked indoors, who no longer knew
what could or should be. In short, I wanted to forget as quickly as
possible the nakedness of his features a moment before, and the
nakedness of my own body. Nothing had happened and nothing could
– just an old uncle and a girl growing into a woman.

Confused, I stood above the basin. I did not know how to leave,
how to say that I knew nothing and wanted to know nothing, that I
would not pester him again or come here again. And then he extended
his hand – everything in that little room was within arm's length – and
drew me to him. In his eyes there were weariness, sadness and resig-
nation. There was nothing left in them of that earlier lust. The pale old
eyes were wreathed with fans of little lines.

After that, the water occasionally splashed from the basin as I hurried down the icy passage. My left hand now held on to my attic door
and carefully shut the bolt. The door, that utterly irreplaceable door,
divided me from everything, even from the strangely cheerful gaze of
Frau Jastrow, who followed my progress along the passage, leaning
against the door jamb of my recent refuge.

A few weeks later, they found a bunk for me in the home for girls
aged between fourteen and eighteen, the *Mädchenheim*, and the dis-
tasteful episode in the house on Q Street faded.

Mädchenheim

They called it L 410. Why not simply call it the Girls' Home, that yellow-coloured house, built at the end of the last century, situated to the right of the church on the square in Terezín? During World War II, a community of approximately 300 girls lived in this building, formerly the headquarters of the army garrison. The streets in Terezín at that time did not have sensible names. They were known by numbers, each prefixed with either L or Q.

The girls in L 410 arrived and departed as new transports came and went. Those for whom no place could be found were packed into dormitories in civilian houses and in barracks with the adults.

The 300 girls made up a diverse community. Some were beautiful, some were average; some were gifted, others were not. Some were kind, even in extraordinarily difficult circumstances, some were ... not kind. For me, after the distress I had endured in the house on Q Street, L 410 was absolute paradise. For several months I had been hidden in the attic in Q Street without having been listed on any registers. I had had the advantages of privacy and a bolt on the inside of my door. But I had also had the disadvantages of loneliness, a layer of frost on my face in the early mornings and the cries that reached me from the floors below. That house had emitted such sighs and anguished screams. As each morning approached, it had been filled with the unbearable atmosphere of death, and corpses lay on the landing above the stairs ready to be taken away. Leaving the house involved walking round those liberated by death.

Let me explain how I came to L 410. I had met Šany (Alexandr) Singer through my father when they both lived in the Sudeten Barracks, after father had been 'adopted' by a group of carpenters. They were young men who had gathered around a cabaret artist, Karel Švenk (who would subsequently die in Auschwitz).

Šany Singer, whose family came from Carpathian Ruthenia, was a marvellous tenor. He was then about twenty-four years old, small, with a face like a full moon and kind brown eyes. He had a great sense of humour and, later, when the conductor Rafael Schächter produced *The Bartered Bride*, the role of Vašek suited him perfectly. Early in 1943, the inimitable Šany became my saviour because, somehow – I still do not know how – he arranged a place for me in room number 15 in the *Mädchenheim*. It was his misfortune to be attracted to me at first sight, but the attraction was not mutual. In spite of this he became a good friend and, as he survived, we met again after the war. He was always interested in my life and I in his. Years later, in 1968, he was to emigrate from Prague to South Africa with his wife and children, in order to further his career as a cantor in the synagogue.

During the first few days of my change from the house of the aged to the house of the young, I was very insecure. Before all this, I had only lived at home. How should I now behave, how would I mix with the girls? Would they accept me? I didn't know. But joy conquered anxiety, for I now was where only a few could be. There were thousands of girls in Terezín and just a few hundred places in the *Mädchenheim*. Bunks became vacant only when their occupants received notice to join a transport to the east.

Former garrison offices had been transformed into the typical Terezín living quarters and included the ground floor, the two floors above it, and even the attic. Every metre was utilised for three-tiered bunks of roughly sawn timber. We got splinter after splinter if we climbed carelessly from one bunk to another. In the middle of the room, or wherever there was any space, stood a table and, if we were lucky, some chairs.

We had our things, clothes and spare clogs, in suitcases under our bunks. Tin plates, a few bits and pieces from the past – dolls, a teddy bear, a family photograph taken on a Sunday by the river – were on a shelf above your bunk. Each bunk was 70 centimetres wide and 170 centimetres long. Tall or large girls had little comfort. After a few weeks of living there, however, they adjusted to that width. The rectangular space of the bunk offered the only privacy, a borrowed privacy in borrowed time.

The lack of cupboards didn't bother us. The suitcases for our few clothes from home were quite sufficient. The one or two books which we had illegally included in the allowed 50 kilos were under our mattresses. We also folded trousers or skirts carefully under the mattress if they needed ironing. It worked. Muddy overalls were hung on a nail on the bunk.

The wish to have a variety of clothing was resolved communally in our room: whatever we had was shared. An order of important occasions was respected. For example, the first rendezvous with a new friend was top of the list when clothes were chosen. Then came a concert or play in the attic or the cellar. Thirdly, there was strolling during the time between finishing work and the curfew. The curfew for all inmates was 8 p.m. in winter and 9 p.m. in summer.

There were about twenty of us, sometimes more, in that not very large room. Sometimes, for a short while after the departure of a transport, there were fewer. None of us spent much time 'at home' anyway. Regulations stipulated that young people must work in the fields and gardens of the SS officers, digging up the hard earth in early spring and so on until harvesting. Children and adults worked the same hours: anything from nine to eleven hours a day. It is said that as long as a man lives, he can bear a heavy cross. But no, not like this. There was too much hopelessness. Harvesting sugar beet – pulling it out of the wet earth with bare hands – was a hard slog. Yet sometimes, returning from work, we even felt frolicsome. We were stumbling from exhaustion but even so we whispered about the handsome boy who stood on the dray that took the sugar beet to the factory, and speculated about what we could do to attract his attention. In other words, we were ordinary girls and even in those grim conditions we lived our own lives. In all the bunks, at every level, pillow fights about boys, about differing opinions, or just for fun, were the stuff of life and gave us the strength to go on living.

We Terezín children had already experienced what it meant to live with our parents in barracks, with adults and with old and sick people. The despair of our parents, about the fate of their children, their own parents, and themselves – despair resulting from their inability to change anything – was enormous. The emotional state of the adults was shaken more deeply than ours. They experienced the loss of homes, security and faith so much more keenly than we. Their lives, ideals, moral standards, self-confidence and hope for the future were totally threatened. The moral, emotional and mental core of these human beings had been damaged – sometimes irreparably. The adults had to come to terms not only with their own problems but also with those of strangers who, in such proximity, endured similar despair. No one had previously experienced living together in such overcrowded and cramped conditions. People helped each other, but they also irritated each other, then insulted, abused and, undoubtedly, hated each other. In Terezín living quarters, family life, face to face with other families, acquired a new dimension: it was a struggle for individuals to save scraps of human dignity once their bodies and souls had been laid bare.

A Terezín child was a mirage – a child who had been excluded from society. According to the Nuremberg Laws, enforced in Czechoslovakia since early in the German occupation, a Jewish child was forbidden to go to school, to a park, on a train or bus, to a cinema or a gymnasium, to play with other children or have a cat or a dog. Even before deportation to Terezín, this child had to wear a yellow star above her heart with JUDE printed on it. This child had also had to be well behaved at home, if only because family worries should not be exacerbated.

A typical Terezín child did not know the text books from the class that she or he should have attended. But because of a few men and women, most of whom did not themselves survive, about one hundred Terezín children survived with a wide general knowledge and a sound education. And, what's even more important, they survived with a sense of morality, a knowledge of what constituted a decent human being.

The Jewish Council of Elders, the *Ältestenrat*, had a department for young people, the *Jugendfürsorge*. The desperate plight of children and youth inspired several exceptional people in this department to come up with an audacious idea. They approached the German authorities and requested the establishment of hostels for young people of different ages, at least for a few hundred children. With all the movement in Terezín, the coming and going of thousands of people, many buildings were vacant and were available for such a purpose.

Luckily, the Nazis did not understand that this was an attempt to save, both physically and spiritually, the youngest Jewish generation. It was an attempt to withdraw a few hundred children from a sad and complicated adult environment. Several devoted people, committed educators, formulated their goals: to uphold children's confidence in life, in people, and not to allow them to live without hope, or fall into moral decay and despair: above all, to educate them, to teach them whatever was possible. Their education had been disrupted and some of them had not even finished primary school. None of those enthusiastic people, those teachers, could have known that of the fifteen thousand children who passed through the Terezín ghetto, so few would survive. Yet I think that even if they had known, they would have behaved in just the same way. Because of their determination and effort, the *Mädchenheim*, the *Knabenheim* (Boys' Home) and even a *Kindergarten* were established.

Our house-mother in the *Mädchenheim* was one of these exceptional people, Rósa Engländerová. She had come to Terezín with her husband and their daughter Rája in January 1942. As a young student, she had studied psychology and wanted to devote her life to young people. It was an irony that she began this work in Terezín. Quite early on, her husband was listed on a 'work transport' for the east, but she remained in Terezín with her twelve-year-old daughter. When she acquired her straw mattress in the Hamburg Barracks, well before the *Mädchenheim* had been established, she did all that was possible (and close to impossible) for the children there, so that they would not be devastated by the wretched conditions, the hunger, filth and despair. She did not allow idleness. She stimulated them into activity. She taught them everything she knew, and she found co-workers who, like her, wanted the children to preserve their faith in the future. The department dealing with young people could not have made a better decision than when they entrusted the *Mädchenheim* to her.

'Mrs Rósa' selected her colleagues carefully. There was only one young man in this enclave of women, Willy Groag. He was a man who exuded reassurance, quiet strength and equanimity, such important characteristics in an extremely complex environment. Willy Groag and the other carers, mostly women not much older than their protégées, did everything they could to ensure that we would not lose hope. The faith and hope in survival were important so that we would want to learn whatever our voluntary teachers offered: the history of mankind, and art, painting, music, literature, Czech and Hebrew. They hoped that whatever we learned would last not only for a few hours or days but for our whole lives. Mrs Rósa wanted her staff to fight for the mental and spiritual strength of girls who were threatened both physically and psychologically. It was a daily, tiring struggle for the girls, many of whom had lost faith in humanity and in any reason for living. How could the staff teach them to live for the present and achieve a quality of life? How could one persuade them that they had a future?

Above all, the *Mädchenheim* had to have rules, strict guidelines as to what was allowed and what was not allowed. It was difficult to explain to children and to adolescents who had already lived under imposed constraints outside the ghetto for several years that even here, in this relatively sheltered cell, the *Heim* which was now our home, rules and regulations were necessary. Each room had its carer, some of whom were very young, only a little older than the girls. They had to fight us, fight our aversion to rules of any sort, especially here. We often protested and sometimes nagged at our carers that the strict rules of the home augmented the strict prison regulations of the ghetto. But how else could tidiness, cleanliness and order be maintained in an environment where all known values and principles were being ignored? Only now do I understand what obstacles our carers, our older friends, had to overcome.

The Jewish leaders divided us up into rooms according to our age. This was not always adhered to, as the placing of as many girls as possible in the *Mädchenheim* was the main aim. So experiences of life, both good and bad, were soon passed on from older girls to younger ones. We grew up very quickly.

I like to remember all the positive things that happened in the *Mädchenheim*. We studied there, we learned so much, and I think that in some ways we were given a better education, even if it was limited, than we would have got in a normal school during the Nazi occupation. But it was not just a formal education. There were also the many other ways in which our carers influenced us. I was very fond of Kamila Rosenbaumová, the carer in our room 15. Kamila was an honest, sincere, energetic woman who did not spoil us. We knew she liked us. She did everything she could to ensure that we kept high personal standards – to be clean and tidy, stay in good spirits and foster good relationships with those around us.

Kamila's language was a little coarse. But she said everything so naturally, and with such charm, that she could say what she liked. I think we all admired her enormously. She was certainly a person whom I valued greatly and I was friends with her for years after the war, until she died. We found her interesting. She had been a dancer and imposed her artistic discipline on us. As a dancer she had worked in the Liberated Theatre and she knew songs by the pre-war Czech playwrights Voskovec and Werich. She shared with us her theatre memories, all of them still vivid. It was wonderful to have her. I recall that sometimes we were lazy about cleaning our room, but Kamila did not let us get away with it. Now I know how important it was that she did not allow us to wallow in dirt, as thousands of lice and fleas would have eaten us alive.

Zdenka Müllerová was another carer responsible for our spiritual and physical development. My memories of her are positive, but not as concrete as my memories of Kamila. My most significant recollection of her is that in late May 1945, just after the war, I ran across her in the centre of Prague. I knew that after having been imprisoned in Terezín she had been deported to Auschwitz. It was a miracle to meet someone who had been taken away but had returned from that death camp. More importantly, she told me something that was almost unbelievable. I asked her, as I asked everyone from 'there', whether she had come across my grandmother in Auschwitz.

Zdenka told me, 'Yes, I saw her there. She stood behind the wire fence and called out to ask, as we had just come from Terezín, if anyone knew Renuška Friesová. I went closer to her and whispered that yes, I knew Renka and had seen her just a few days ago. Your grandmother had tears in her eyes and cried with happiness that she had news of you.'

I almost fainted. I did not expect anything like that. Zdenka inspired in me a flicker of hope. As she had seen my grandmother six months before the end of the war, perhaps Grandmother would return. But she did not, my dear little grandmother.

Thanks to our carers and teachers, we girls from the *Mädchenheim* and boys from the *Knabenheim* found a source of strength within ourselves and developed an attitude that ensured our survival. Attitude was absolutely important. Our frame of mind gave us vital optimism, even if it was inexplicable and almost incomprehensible. Most of the adults knew or expected what was to come. Perhaps we also knew, but we successfully prevented the intrusion of anxiety and fear into our peer relationships, and into those with our teachers and carers. What our teachers and carers did for us was remarkable.

Irena Krausová, a beautiful twenty-four-year-old, was the carer in room number 25. Full of optimism and with a zest for life, she inspired everyone around her and became a model for all the teachers, even those older than she. Her presence was sufficient to dispel sadness and hopelessness. Her teaching plans and methods were well thought out, she knew how to express her ideas clearly, and she taught the girls with humour and fun. It was obvious to Irena that she could win us over by her own example.

Working with us adolescents was not easy. We had been tossed unmercifully into the role of prisoners without rights behind the ramparts. Often, we looked on helplessly as a loved one was squeezed into a cattle wagon which, secured and sealed, left for the unknown.

Irena and the other carers made sure that, even in this environment where self-preservation was a basic desire, we shared everything and did not steal as much as a crumb of *Mädchenheim* bread. The bread ration was ridiculous. The regular menu for the morning was a tin bowl of black slops, at noon a bowl of thin soup or a ladle of fake *sauerkraut* made from turnips, or three half-rotten unpeeled potatoes with a sort of gravy, and on Fridays a piece of cake covered with thin custard. In the evenings, even thinner soup.

In spite of this, we girls never once had to be punished for stealing food in the home – possibly because, as far as I can remember, none was to be found! Among the adults living in the barracks, on the other hand, the theft of food, and probably other things, occurred often. But who were we to cast the first stone? Occasionally one of us would receive a parcel from outside, if there was anyone left to send one. A half-kilogram parcel daily was allowed. Five hundred grams could fit into a small box and whoever received one was happy – not only for the food but more so for the ever-important endearments and reassurances the box also contained. I sampled this pleasure for a few months before the Germans imprisoned Grandmother, Grandfather and, eventually, Uncle Vilík.

Our carers had to deal with the enormous problem of whether they had the right to ask us to share the little we received with everyone in our room. Most of the girls had no one on the outside to send them anything. The decision was left to each of us, either to share, or guiltily nibble the goodies alone and in secret. On the whole, we divided up the parcels. But the sources gradually dried up and only very occasionally did anyone receive a parcel.

Irena and the other carers disciplined our selfishness and the greed for self-preservation. But her own life was to end tragically. It was autumn, 1944. The end of the war was almost within reach. Just a few more months ... About a thousand people a day were leaving in cattle wagons from the Terezín ghetto. For some time it had been suspected that the transports led to a place of extermination. But how could one really imagine platforms at Auschwitz, from where people went directly to the gas chambers? It really could not seem possible. So we remained in the dark – nobody knew anything, those things could not happen, surely the world would not tolerate it?

The summons to go was a narrow strip of thin paper, with a name, a tag number, tomorrow's date (it always came the day before), the time – usually four in the morning – and the place of assembly. Those narrow strips were often distributed only a few hours before departure. There was no time for anything. It was forbidden to be out at night, so on the other side of the ghetto one's family did not know. But because girls in the *Mädchenheim* were all together, we knew who was condemned. We helped each other pack and put some food together, or perhaps wrote a poem for those who were leaving. Above all, we extended love and friendship to them. On those damp autumn mornings, when some of the girls walked through the bleak Terezín streets on a journey with an end which was fortunately unforeseen, we, their closest friends, accompanied them. We tried to get through the gate of the barracks where the railway siding ended. A few hours later, we tried to get as far as the platform. Those who were not wily and swift enough to avoid the soldiers and SS officers could find themselves in a cattle wagon as well. Unless the last wagon was bursting at the seams, the soldiers wildly and gleefully combed the barracks, chased, caught and deported whoever was around. Once, by a whisker, I avoided that by hiding in a garbage bin.

One October day, Irena accompanied her mother and her friends to the wagon. That autumn was a fatal season for thousands of Jews. The German headquarters wanted to begin the liquidation of Terezín quietly and in an orderly fashion, without resistance from its inmates. Soon, the time came even for the few hundred children living in the homes. Most of their parents had already disappeared. SS Obersturmführer Rahm, the ghetto commander, summoned the leaders of the girls' and boys' homes to inform them that the homes would be abolished. He said that most of the carers would leave on the transports with the children, so that they could care for them at their new location. Irena was chosen to stay with the remaining children in Terezín.

Before the transport left, Irena and some others managed to sneak through the barracks gate and spend the rest of the night in a huge, barn-like room with a thousand women waiting on their straw mattresses for the dawn, when the train to collect them would be coupled up. Irena wanted to help those who, after such a terrible night, were weak and could hardly move. She went with them right to the wagons. The last wagon was already sealed shut and Irena was about to leave the platform, her head bent, her eyes filled with tears. At that moment somebody roughly grabbed her shoulder.

'What are you doing here, you want to disappear, eh?' The SS guard, named Heindl, eagerly dragged her to an officer. Without a word, the officer pointed his finger to the wagon. The guard undid the seal and Irena Krausová disappeared forever with a thousand other women. I watched this scene in horror, impotent and angry, from the barred window of the barracks cellar. That scene was so tragic that no theatre could ever stage it.

That was autumn 1944: the end of the idyll at the *Mädchenheim*.

Only about a hundred of us ever returned to the post-war world and we remember with gratitude those two years of the home's existence. It enabled hundreds of girls, during their imprisonment in Terezín, to live a life of joy and laughter for at least a few months, and that counterbalanced the miserable reality. Youth has a different approach to death from adults. In its own way, as death comes closer for young people, it seems more remote. I was young.

Also, we were not as preoccupied with worries about the future as the adults. Our feelings were constantly being challenged, in friendship and in love. Partings caused by the hostility and might of strangers were our daily experience. Because of that, love took on a dimension that normal life cannot give it. Moments of joy were as staggering as moments of despair. We had to learn to live in the present, and we did, because our future was unknown.

Nowadays, most people in the world know fleas and bedbugs only from biology texts. We knew them intimately, without exaggeration, as a personal experience. In trench-like conditions, among overcrowded humans, these tiny insects are difficult to combat. How did we cope with that plague with which everybody in the ghetto struggled?

After a day's exhausting work, we slept so soundly that even the concentrated attack of whole regiments of hungry, dexterous and uncatchable insects did not wake us. In the morning, some of us, particularly those with sweeter blood, which included me, had swollen shapeless masses instead of faces. The girls mischievously presented mirrors to each other.

'Hey, look at yourself, what a beauty! Do you have a date tonight? Will your sweetheart see you in the fields this morning?'

The bedbugs and fleas were not selective; we were all affected one way or another. We laughed so much at our appearance that the three-tiered bunks would shake.

Someone came up with an idea which we wholeheartedly welcomed. We would have a competition. Bedbugs are red, with lots of legs, and as they crawl inside the linen you cannot catch them on your body. After being squashed, they leave a red mark and a really unbelievably disgusting stink. Their bites last several days. They are so revolting that we did not admit them to our contest. But fleas, they're another story. They are like jolly, black spots which, if in good condition, can jump as high as half a metre. It is an art to catch them. We found some empty pill and match boxes and, morning or evening, caught fleas in our blankets. The drowsy fleas delighted in sleeping after the nightly feast on our bodies. We promised each other that we would not cheat when counting them, as we carefully put them into the little boxes. The winner – whoever caught the most – received a valuable prize: a slice of bread.

Surprisingly, and with only a few exceptions, we had neither head nor clothes lice, as we were able to maintain personal cleanliness most of the time. In the adults' quarters, chiefly those of elderly people, lice were a calamity because they transmitted diseases – worst of all, typhus.

An adult drawn unjustly, forcibly and innocently into this plight simply could not react farcically to the horror, humiliation and pain caused by these insects. It would have been insane if anyone had expected that. The adults had to mobilise their strength to defend themselves against the insects as best they could and to hide their despair from strangers with whom they lived, slept and excreted in such close confinement. If there was a glut of insects, about once every six months, we were moved out for two or three days and L 410 was disinfected. This was to our leaders' credit. But the most effective disinfectant in the home was our speciality – laughter, laughter and more laughter.

The book *Children's Drawings and Poems* (Prague, 1959) includes this small poem:

> A little mouse sits in her nest
> Chasing a flea in her coat.
> She cannot catch it,
> It has burrowed into her fur.
> She chases it round and round –
> A flea is a nasty creature.
>
> Along comes her father,
> He scratches her coat,
> Catches the flea in a twinkle
> Then cooks it in a pot.
> The mouse announces to Grandpa:
> 'We have a flea for tea'.

A hot summer night. Almost no air moved through the windows of room 15 and you felt you could *slice* the heat and darkness. In the overheated blackness, the touch of a blanket or another sweaty body was unbearable. It was late and lights had been out for some time, but we could hear each other toss and turn and we could not fall asleep. The battle with darkness and heat felt intolerable.

From time to time, the wooden planks of the badly nailed bunks creaked. I became aware of someone crawling over the girl next to me. After months of having been on what we called 'the ground floor' I finally lived on the third level of bunks. The greatest advantage about this was that no one slept above you. The girl who crawled her way across the others towards me could only be my friend Alena. It was an unwelcome prospect because I really did not want to be roused from the light, half-sleepy, half-dreamy state that transported my body and mind through space.

Alenka (Alena) gently pushed me and pressed herself against me. I moved away slightly, but at the same time did not want her to notice that. I knew how sensitive she was and how much she needed love. Alenka had always been a loner, and her first weeks in the *Mädchenheim*, before I arrived there, had been terribly unhappy, introspective and morose.

Now, in this stifling night, I was naked, but I reached for the flannel nightdress under my pillow and hurriedly pulled it over my head. I had no other nightdresses. We had left home in winter, it had seemed a waste of space to include summer things, and anyway, by summer ...

Such long nights without light, and without the possibility of going out in the summer evenings, attracted the girls to each other like magnets. They visited each other's 'sovereign territory'. They were gentle, and they compensated for the absence of their parents' love. They whispered their most secret longings. It was a mysterious world, and only here and there was some lonely soul not permitted entry. Friendship at this vulnerable age is only a step away from love and resembles it very closely. It is jealous and passionate, it wants all and forgives nothing. It can also come to be regarded as the most important connection to life.

I liked Alenka, but she *loved* me. If I did not know it then, I know it now. She was serious, gentle and always a bit sad. Her family were somewhere in Terezín but I never saw them. She had a younger brother but she did not get on with him or with her parents.

To tolerate her in the burning oven of my bed, I had to imagine her huge, round, velvety dark eyes, her very long eyelashes and her white-porcelain complexion. One of her legs was slightly shorter than the other. Alenka limped, and no one, not even I, dared hurt her. Her long, curly black hair fell like tiny snakes onto her narrow shoulders. It hid her unclean neck. That beautiful, slender neck was covered by impetigo.

Impetigo was an integral part of life in Terezín, facilitated by bedbugs, fleas, head lice and dirt. It appears as small, almost unnoticeable blisters anywhere on a person's body. The blisters burst and, for weeks, fester into tiny oozing sores. Sometimes the sores merge into whole patches. Uncleanliness, under-nourishment, heat, sweat and lack of medical attention contribute to the presence of impetigo. Scratching causes it to spread and become infected. Only a strong will helps someone to withstand the pain and avoid scratching the festering sores. Cleanliness helps, but the conditions in Terezín naturally made this difficult to achieve.

Alenka did not have a strong will and she did not like the cold water which was all we had. I had tried coaxing her, warning her that she would lose my friendship, but nothing helped. Secretly, she ravaged her white skin with dirty little nails, although she was ready to swear that she had not touched her body. But the reasons why I could not fulfil my threats were stronger than my distaste.

All these thoughts raced through my mind in those few moments. I struggled with my aversion when she pressed her lips to my ear and softly whispered some lines from Paul Verlaine.

> Autumn pastures are beautiful to gaze upon
> but cows that graze there are slowly eating poison –
> saffron blooms, the colour of your eyelids.
> Beneath your eyes are pale half-moons
> coloured like saffron blooms
> and slowly I eat the poison from your eyes.

Alenka's voice was like the most beautiful music but her body was repulsive to me. I lacked the strength, however, to push her away. I didn't know how to tell her to go and take a shower in the

107

cold bathroom – cold even now in summer. Something which was a privilege for me, to shower daily under a stream of water, was agony for her. Anyway, whatever I said would have been even more painful for her than an icy shower.

The verse she chose was only too clear-sighted. It expressed exactly what was forming within me. Yes, poison. Those two syllables overwhelmed me. Poison, slowly killing, visually and verbally, slowly penetrating everything. Countries, cities, the ghetto. Poison, threatening everything and everybody. Taking not only life but also joy and beauty, and supplanting them with destructive substitutes. Poisoning everything and not permitting a mignonette or a rose to fill the spring countryside with their scent. I was only fifteen. Is it a little? Is it a lot?

Noise, laughter and cheerful banter gradually swelled above the words and verses which Alenka was whispering in my ear. Neither she nor I had noticed that the whole room was now awake and in high spirits. The girls argued or, rather, squabbled about the day's topic.

Often, when we lay in the dark and could not sleep, we chose a topic which we would discuss. Sometimes we related fables, sometimes family stories, and at other times experiences of the previous day. Today's topic woke me up completely. It was 'How I lost my virginity'.

'Now, one after the other, from the lower bunk upwards, and no one can drop out!' someone shouted. 'But don't lie, girls. Firstly, it doesn't matter and, secondly, we know all about each other anyway and we would see through any lies!'

This topic was the last thing we needed – I as well as Alena. I thought to myself, 'We will both plunge into big trouble, dear Alenka ...' But I whispered in her ear, 'Don't worry, before it reaches this level of the bunks, it'll cease to amuse them and they'll go to sleep.'

Suddenly it was quiet and someone below us shyly and quietly began speaking.

Most of the girls had their first sexual experience here in Terezín. They were neither happy nor joyful experiences. It always happened hurriedly in the wrong place and certainly at the wrong time. There were just too many people in such a small space. If there was love, Love's bed was like Juliet's tomb. Lovers were always torn apart, not by hatred between Montagues and Capulets, but by a single sentence on a strip of paper: the call to a transport.

Most girls believe that their first sexual experience is something important, something that should be beautiful. This, of course, doesn't always occur, even under normal circumstances. But how and where could it happen here in Terezín? In a deserted alleyway beneath the ramparts behind the Cavalier Barracks?

The Cavalier Barracks housed the mentally ill. Although transports regularly took away its residents, this last home for those wretched people was always full. From the barred windows one could hear groans, screams, cries and the sounds accompanying fights. What a strange melody to accompany the act of consummation between two young people! But apart from those sounds, and the desperate staring faces and twisted hands gripping the bars, it was fairly quiet.

Or perhaps sex happened another way, in a bunk in the men's barracks. The men created privacy with a curtain of hessian. There was enough hessian because everything brought into Terezín was in sacks. A little curtain was pulled around the bunk. Obviously, life beyond the curtain went on as normal. In the Sudeten Barracks, the rooms were so large that up to a hundred men could fit on the three tiers of bunks. With a considerable effort of the imagination, it was possible to think of this bunk as a royal bed with a canopy. After all, kings and queens had intercourse in the presence of their courtiers. Unfortunately, such a comparison did not occur to me, so I simply rejected the experience. My rejection of it was neither meritorious nor honourable (though in our circumstances these terms were ridiculously inappropriate), but that's how it was for me, for Alenka and a few others.

But what we did experience – virgins or not, girls and boys, indeed everyone from childhood to old age – were endless partings in which there was little hope of a reunion. Fishermen's wives in Scandinavia also said farewell to their husbands who were going to sea in fragile boats. They never knew if a father, a husband or a son would return. But there *was* a difference. Their menfolk went out for their livelihood, voluntarily. In Terezín, love always ended; he went, she went, on the May ... October ... transport. There was not even time to break up, as adolescent relationships do, with the capriciousness of youth.

As I listened to the girls' stories, all of this was passing through

109

my mind. I pressed closer to Alena and forgot about the sores covering her body. It seemed that nobody was sleeping and the storytellers were inexorably approaching the third level.

Hanka, a little older, seventeen, laughed bitterly at herself. She, just like the others, was glad in the sense that she could reveal the dissatisfaction of her experience. She tried to be cynical, but she ended up with tears in her voice.

'All that remains is a stained skirt I can't bear to look at. Does anyone want it, girls?'

After living together for those few weeks, we knew each other very well. Better, indeed, than we ever knew our parents or brothers and sisters.

Again my thoughts wandered. How relative time is here! It shrinks and expands according to the circumstances. In one week, you could know more happiness, love and joy than in years of freedom. In one week you could find true love, experience it and then lose it. With just minutes before separation in the transportees' collection area in the barracks, where you sat holding hands on a mattress with your Romeo, imprinting his face in your mind forever, you could endure the seemingly endless suffering of parting. He, whom you were so sure was the 'real one', and 'for ever' – he was leaving. 'For ever' lasted a few days, or weeks, or for some even months. Thirty days is seven hundred and twenty hours, seven hundred and twenty hours is forty-three thousand two hundred minutes. Then, it equalled infinity. And when a beloved left, a new week, minutes, hours began again – another era. You had to live through it. A new love 'for ever' replaced the vanished one. That did not happen to me. The sadness of partings distressed me for months.

In the girls' stories, so recently lived through, there was less of passion and more of bitterness. There was some happiness, but more disappointment and indifference. Often bleak reality – that was the saddest. Alenka, always over-sensitive, began to shake feverishly. What should she say, for God's sake what could she say? She could neither invent a story nor confess her virginity. She was convinced that no one would look at her because she limped and was ugly ... It was not true. That white, fragile porcelain creature was wrong about herself. But there was little time for the right one to embrace her.

I said, 'Don't worry Alenka, I'll rescue you, I'll tell them such a story that they'll die! And it will be so long that they'll fall asleep. Honestly, don't worry!'

At that moment even I had no idea what I would actually say, but I hoped something would occur to me. I would simply make something up.

Only, when it was my turn, without wanting to, I began telling a true story.

'Now I'll tell you a story girls -- how I have stayed a virgin! You wanted a story. OK, you've got it! It's ages ago. I was twelve when the anti-Jewish laws and edicts imprisoned us at home. You know. No one was allowed to make contact with us so that their race wouldn't be contaminated by us. The enforced confinement eased my parents' worries regarding my 'honour'.

'I don't know about you, but it didn't bother me that I couldn't go to school. I took it quite calmly that the end of my formal schooling was around grade five. I read everything that I could find. These were cowboy stories and thrillers kept in our toilet or under Father's pillow. They helped him to fall asleep. I used to take book after book, including those expressly forbidden, from our bookshelves. I gleaned some wisdom, I formed concepts of good and evil, love and hatred, truth and betrayal and I created ideas about what I might possibly experience. So I don't know about you girls, but those edicts didn't affect me very much. I lived in my own world as soon as I had finished the housework. Being forbidden to go to the park? To school? To go out at night? I wouldn't have been allowed anyway! To go shopping only in specified hours? So what?

'Yes, some things were awful: being forbidden to cross the district boundary and use public transport meant that I couldn't visit my lovely grandma and grandpa. The ban on keeping a pet meant taking Miki, my sweet fox terrier, to strangers. They accepted our money, took him in and left him tied up in a kennel. When I rode away on my bicycle he cried so much that I still have nightmares about it.'

'Hey, listen here,' someone said. 'Don't try rambling on, thinking that we'll fall asleep! Get back to the point.'

'Don't worry, I'll get there. It's all relevant so just wait!'

'Well, at home, we lived through the reprisals after Heydrich's assassination. Each day the lists of executions were in the newspaper and on notice-boards. "Executions in the twentieth century? It's impossible!" But it was possible, and getting worse all the time. "Such things cannot happen, they must soon stop, better times lie ahead," said the adults every evening in one of the rooms of our apartment. The authorities had relocated five Jewish families there. In despair, they played canasta every night and discussed the situation from every angle.

'My parents didn't share my complacency about my lack of education. For a few weeks, a matriculation student, whom I fell madly in love with, came to our place, but he soon stopped coming, he was afraid. Unexpectedly, and of his own accord, a young man appeared and rang our doorbell. He was a priest whom I knew by sight. He said to my parents, "It's uncivilised for a gifted child to be deprived of an education. Every Sunday I see her kneeling in church and humbly praying. It is my duty not to leave a young soul uneducated. I am offering to teach her, since she is a baptised Catholic."

'The next day, I went through the familiar big presbytery gates. Damaged stucco walls lined the entrance-way of old, worn cobblestones. A howling wind swept from the courtyard. It had been arranged that I would come in the evening after five. Darkness fell early, no one would see me. After eight we were not allowed outside, but by then I would be home again. I was always afraid of the dark and here, behind the gate, you could hardly see. To endure the anxiety that overcame me when I ascended the wide, shallow, wooden stairs, I pretended to be a mysterious pupil of some famous young scholar from the Middle Ages. Instead of the ghost I expected, only a plaster statue of the Virgin Mary and Child – in blue, gold and pink – looked at me from a niche on the landing. The stairs were lit by a candle in front of the statue.

'I felt chilled to the bone. Each creaking step terrified me. Finally, I reached the barred, wooden partition and pulled a rope attached to a little bell. It swung to and fro and rang cheerfully. At the same time, the young and very handsome priest called out heartily, "Welcome, child. Come on in, don't be afraid."

'The heel tips on my shoes clicked impolitely. I tried to tiptoe but the shoes wouldn't bend. The priest looked smart in black, with a white clerical collar. A few months ago, at school, he was quite remote, but now I was here alone with him. In class he had spoken very quietly and no one breathed a word. He'd told us fascinating tales about saints who always fought bravely and were tortured rather than abandon their faith.

'The room we entered was large and whitewashed. There was only a rectangular table with heavy chairs around it and, in the corner, a sort of a stand similar to the one on which our accountant entered his figures into ledgers. In the middle of the ceiling hung an adjustable, plain porcelain shade with a weak light bulb.

'He led me to the stand. Without a word, he helped me off with my coat, took an exercise book from the drawer and said, "We will start with mathematics, I want to see what you know."

'I knew rather little but whatever I did know, I now forgot. After this first lesson I left feeling embarrassed, unhappy and the dumbest person in the world. "I'll not turn up again, never ever," I said to myself. But that wasn't possible and so I went there again and again. I battled with the work – second-year high school level. I would rather have washed all the windows at home. That seemed to me, around then, to be more useful than studying.

'One day, stretching up uncomfortably, I stood at the desk, still barely reaching it. I was working out a most difficult problem. The priest was walking backwards and forwards in the narrow aisle between me and the table, occasionally bumping into me or a chair. I had to use all my strength to concentrate. From time to time he stopped right behind me and looked over my shoulder at my (surely incorrect) calculations.

'I almost cried. Does someone really want to save such a stupid girl from the Nazis' plans? What will he tell my parents? They'll be angry and they'll be right! But to my surprise he said, "Good, good, go on ..." Then silence.

'I held my breath. Something was about to happen. He pressed his body to my back. All of it. Then, from behind, he forcibly embraced me. He squeezed me so tightly that, in pain, I cried out. He grabbed me again and, with astonishing strength which I wouldn't have expected from such a frail person, he lifted me up. He carried me towards a door. I kicked. I probably hit his shin, because he hissed with pain and let me go. For a while, I'm not sure how long, there was a chase around the table and then I was fleeing down the dark stairs, through the pitch-black reception area and outside into the unfriendly streets. It was pouring with rain, there was no one about, even the soldiers weren't at the barracks windows. The fortress town of Josefov is small and in no time at all I was home.

'Soaked to the skin, I thought to myself: "What now, what will I tell my parents? What can I tell them so that I don't have to go there any more?" I was so terribly ashamed – of myself, my body, my behaviour which was such that it apparently sparked lust in a man promised to God. I was also embarrassed for him, as he had taken advantage of our position, my parents' trust and my obvious ignorance. He knew that I wouldn't say anything to anybody and perhaps I wouldn't even have the chance to say anything ... Words, sentences, for and against – everything spun around in my mind. The rain trickling down my face turned salty with tears. "Is it my sin? Yes, it is my fault that I aroused the devil in him."

'You know, girls, now, two years later, I understand things better. But then? I was confused and finally I decided that I would never have anything to do with any man. That decision calmed me a little, so after an hour of the storm raging both outside and inside me, I entered the friendly apartment, well lit behind its blacked-out windows. In spite of not wanting to, I blurted out that I wouldn't ever go to the priest's again.

' "You are a lazy, ungrateful girl. What will become of you?" said my father. I didn't answer. I undressed and went to bed. Surprisingly, the next day neither Father nor anyone else mentioned the matter again. So this bizarre experience protected my virginity. No, I don't want to take that "treasure" to my grave, not at all, but I'd rather lose it somewhere else, not here.'

It was quiet and, contrary to my expectations, nobody laughed at me. That 'foolish' story for my 'experienced' friends had indeed put them all to sleep.

After a while, Hanka, the eldest among us, spoke out into that scorching night: 'Hey, forget about it. As soon as you meet the right one, or at least an almost right one, everything will be fine!'

Fancy that, it all turned out well and, above all, she was right. But Alenka cried quietly in my arms. Life was going to give her no time for meeting her 'right one'. A few weeks later she was transferred and gassed at Auschwitz.

The morning after that mass confession, we awoke to a normal weekday. Our carer, Kamila Rosenbaumová, was a tyrant in the mornings, and chased us with words and a broom to clean up our room before we began the day's work. We older girls had to turn up at a farm on the edge of the ghetto at six o'clock. Usually, women and girls worked in the fields and gardens, while the men were assigned harder duties. They slashed wheat with scythes and pulled laden drays of beet to the sugar refinery. The digging of soil, sowing, planting, harvesting of everything possible from spinach to tomatoes, potatoes, corn and sugar beet, tying wheat into sheaves and threshing it, etc., etc. – all this was done by young women and girls. The positive side to this was that all day in summer and winter we were in the fresh air. We were part of nature and away from the musty ghetto. We were also together and at least could chat among ourselves.

My closest friend outside the home was another Hanka who, being three years older than I, was too old to live there. She was tall and pretty, and in riding boots, a man's jacket and a wide hat, she resembled Jeanette MacDonald, the star of the film *Girl of the Golden West*. Sometimes we crawled into the bushes on the ridge between the fields, buried our noses in the sweet-smelling grass, chewed thyme and looked for four-leafed clovers for good luck. Hanka only had to blink and she found some. I never ever found any, but, anyway, we both had luck enough to survive the war. After those happy moments we joined the long line of people weeding around the sugar beet again. I loathed those endless rows of beet, which were two or more kilometres long.

Out there in the fields we stole whatever we could. Practically everything. We discreetly munched dirty parsley or carrots, nibbled corn and gnawed a raw potato. Almost every day we carried something into the ghetto for our friends – spinach scrunched-up in knee-high socks under the wide trouser-legs of our overalls, tomatoes in our brassieres, or potatoes in our knickers next to our stomachs. The risk was enormous. Out in the fields and on the way to and from the ghetto gate only Czech troops guarded us and some of them turned a blind eye, but we knew that one SS guard, whose name I have forgotten, liked to hide somewhere in the outlying bush and watch us through binoculars. As soon as he saw somebody chewing, or stuffing celery, corn or something else into their underwear, he grabbed his motorbike and appeared on the field. He beat up or dragged away anyone he caught and they never reappeared. Stealing resulted in imprisonment in the Small Fortress, or transportation. And if it was transportation, that was the end.

There were also the Vultures. 'Vultures' was what we called the female SS guards who sometimes unexpectedly waited at the ghetto gate when we were returning from the fields. The hit squad. But more often than not, the Czech troops miraculously knew and warned us. So, next to our three-deep lines as we were marched in from work, quickly dumped vegetables disappeared into the ditch. Then the Vultures futilely groped into our brassieres and trousers. Unfortunately they did sometimes succeed in catching someone.

We always returned to the home dog-tired from work, but our day was far from over. Actually, it was just beginning. We would wash the farm dirt off in troughs with cold running water, change our clothes, and then embark on the most significant task demanded by the home leaders: learning.

Only when looking back can I gauge the skill and enthusiasm of our teachers. They had to deal with adolescents who worked very hard and who were confronted every day by death. Almost all the children in Terezín had grandparents, aunts, uncles and parents there, and many of these relatives died – from malnutrition, despair, typhus, tuberculosis, influenza. In Terezín alone, more than 33,000 people died in three years. Each day, there were mass burials. The corpses were stacked up on two-wheel carts or four-wheel hearses pulled by people to the morgue in the ramparts. We ran into those loads daily. Beneath flapping canvas you could see grey-white arms and legs dangling. And then we came into our quarters and our teachers wanted us to be clean and tidy, to sit down and learn. Really, it was a difficult task. Our leaders, Mrs Rósa, Kamila, Irena, Willy and others, concentrated on the basics – the nurturing of a humane attitude towards those around us, emphasising the need for harmony and an appreciation of beauty for the future. Today it probably sounds weird, that faced with falling into an abyss we secretly smuggled blossoms into the ghetto. But even that was officially forbidden in Terezín.

I regard it as a miracle that the education in our *Mädchenheim* was so effective that we even shared food and gave it to those who, after being ill, were the most needy. How often an embrace and kind words from our carers helped us hold on to life! Love had disappeared, our parents were dragged from us. What future could we expect, why live? The strength of those brave and self-sacrificing women was revealed in crises, and those crises were never ending.

Generally, we looked forward to those two hours, in winter between five o'clock and seven, in summer between six and eight. They were organised like a kind of guidance session – through the arts and literary works. We wrote on every possible material with anything we could; we drew with charcoal from the stoves; sometimes we even found water-colour paints in a parcel from the outside world which had escaped the censor. A celebrated collection of poems and drawings, published worldwide under the title *I Never Saw Another Butterfly* (the title of one of its poems), was solely the work of children from the homes.

A young Prague virtuoso pianist and composer, Gideon Klein, spoke captivatingly to us about music. He was as handsome as he was knowledgeable and so we hung on his words. In 1944 he was annihilated. His sister, Líza Kleinová, who was to survive the war and teach music for years in Prague, also shared her knowledge with us. Our love of theatre was awakened by a charming young actor and director, Jiří Schorch. He told us stories, performed, and in lots of ways allowed us to enter the mysterious world of Czech and international theatre. He even directed *The Lantern,* by Alois Jirásek, writing out nearly the whole script from memory. He too was annihilated in 1944.

Mrs Mühlsteinová taught us Czech grammar. She and her three children would also be exterminated. Kamila Rosenbaumová, our carer, not only waved her broom at us but shared with us all aspects of her theatrical past as dancer and choreographer. Her husband and their two children were annihilated, but she, miraculously, survived. Irenka Stadlerová, Friedl Brandejsová, Zdenka Müllerová, and Tela whose surname eludes me – these were more of these courageous and unselfish women. Most of them perished, and we did not even know the names of many others. They came, they worked, they disappeared, never to return. They all taught us to value each moment of life, to cherish each morsel of happiness even in these dreadful conditions. They protected us and with all their strength encouraged us not to lose hope. By example, they taught us not to panic in a catastrophe.

On 16 November 1943 the weather was unseasonably wet and cold. That evening, the German headquarters issued an order that at 5 a.m. the next day all residents of the Terezín ghetto – including the elderly, the children, the disabled and ill – were to line up on a field outside the town. Those who could not walk were to be carried. There was to be a census of all people, as the authorities had no idea of the number of residents.

Rumours flew around Terezín. Nobody knew how many of us were still here after the numerous transports to Auschwitz. Somebody, somehow, 'definitely' knew that, once we were in the field, planes would fly over and bomb us and the world would never know what happened on that dark November morning.

All of us lined up in the rain for the march, which everyone believed was a death march. The freezing damp penetrated our flimsy coats. I do not know how many kilometres we marched to that valley, through unfamiliar and, until now, forbidden territory. Then we stood there, and stood and stood. Many dropped. Some died. But the plane that flew above us for hours and hours did not drop any bombs. Why? What were the intentions of our masters for these tens of thousands of people? Nobody knows.

We returned, exhausted, to our bunks, and in the days that followed, our carers announced an instructive and psychologically sound task: everybody had to write about their feelings that night. It was an attempt to rid us of the nightmare by making us express ourselves. One of those yellowing sheets was later salvaged, the description by thirteen-year-old Rája Engländerová, daughter of Mrs Rósa. Here is what she wrote.

Home, room 25, Rája Engländerová, 13 years old.

17 November 1943 *5 a.m.! We are standing in the courtyard of our Girls' Home and we are freezing. It is a dank, dark, unpleasant, autumn day. The icy wind pelts our faces with rain. We are waiting for our turn to join the long procession of people, guarded by soldiers on both sides. We are going who knows where, apparently for a census.*

At last the gate opens and we are leaving. A soldier with a cruel face and a bayonet at the ready marches next to me. One step out of line and ... We approach the big, black gate which we entered two years ago. On it is a sign, Arbeit macht frei *(Work liberates). The gate swings open. The road is clear. Where to?*

With childlike joy we embrace with our eyes the broad countryside, the fields and, in the distance, forests and a tiny village. We don't think about the fact that this journey may be our last. 'Into a beautiful land, into a beloved land'. I recall the words of Karel Hynek Mácha [the greatest Czech romantic poet, 1810–36] which we had recited in our room only a few days ago. 'Into a beautiful land, into a beloved land' is a cruel irony when confronted with the stony face of the soldier. In his expression I can see it written: we are going to bury you in your beautiful land, very soon. The road ahead of us winds like a snake and we, like black shadows, go on and on.

We arrive at a large meadow, or rather a huge, grassy, crater-like area, which looks as if it were created for the elimination of 30,000 people. They jostle us here and there until we are standing in endless rows, apparently so they can count us better. The SS guards walk among us with sticks in their hands and count. From time to time, they hit someone across the face or they knock someone down to the ground. Then they drop out of sight. Above our heads, a large silver plane appears. It circles just above us and we can clearly see its swastika. It guards us: 30,000 defenceless people, mainly women and children, the old and sick. A few weeks ago, all the menfolk were hauled away in transports to 'labour camps'! What is the significance of being surrounded by soldiers with submachine guns?

It is by now 12 noon. Nothing is happening. We are trying to give the old people courage. We sing softly, whisper to each other and, with all our strength, assist our carers to try and combat the increasing despair of the elderly. During the afternoon, a self-important dandy in a green uniform occasionally walks through our rows, lashing out here and there with a stick. Then it is quiet again. The only sound is the circling plane above us.

We are hungry. It is 5, 6, 7 in the evening. Eight, 9, 10. It has begun to rain. The plane circles relentlessly. Everyone's nerves are at breaking point. Now and then there is a cry when someone falls, or there are despairing petty squabbles. What will they do with us? Nobody knows, all that we can do is wait – and wait. Little children cry with hunger and cold. We try to hide those who have fainted, because we fear for them.

Standing and waiting, for almost 24 hours already. Standing and waiting. Waiting and not thinking. The impenetrable darkness slowly descends on 30,000 traumatised people. It is 11 at night. We are slowly getting used to the idea that we will be here the whole night. Suddenly someone shouts, 'Now they will shoot us with machine guns from the plane!' He is opposed by a stream of despairing protests. No, we will not give the Nazis the pleasure of seeing us frightened and begging! We, from room 25, hold each other's hands and, at that moment, we are friends for life – or death. It is 12 o'clock, midnight. We all know that we cannot last much longer, and that only a miracle can save us. From the valley a thunderous voice is heard: 'Clear the valley, immediately!'

Suddenly the soldiers are here to steer the panicking crowd back to town. A terrible crush builds up. In the darkness everyone fights for his own life and ruthlessly steps on those who have fallen down. Taut nerves give way and people behave like lunatics. Was that the Nazis' intention? An avalanche of people surges forward and the howling laughter of the SS guards accompanies it.

Finally, a few people have the presence of mind to assume control and give orders. First of all, they try to free the children. They instruct us to hold hands firmly, and they clear a path for us. At last we emerge from the throng. Soon we are near the ghetto gates and we run through rows of soldiers who grimace at us, looking like grim reapers in the light of lanterns. We are so scared. 'Los, los', quicker, quicker, shout out rough voices. With the last ounce of strength, we complete the run through the lines of soldiers into the town. We make our way through the gloomy, desolate streets as if in a dream. Somewhere, far behind, we can feel the movement of hordes of people. Completely exhausted, we fall without undressing into our bunks. Merciful sleep engulfs us.

What was it? Why was it? Nothing – only a trifling, practical joke of the Germans on 17 November 1943.

I too wrote my experiences of that night of horror but I do not have those notes now. Thirteen-year-old Rája succeeded in saying a lot. Not everything though. We do not know how many hundreds did not return from that field – how many were stricken by, or trodden to, death. How many died in the following days from the effects of exhaustion? We do not know. There really were no accurate figures about the number of residents either before or after the event. What is certain is that that night, which was like a rehearsal for Hell, undoubtedly reduced the number of Terezín inmates.

In 1943, I lived through a huge typhoid epidemic in Terezín without becoming ill. But forgetting it is impossible. It was one of the most difficult tests of endurance in the girls' home.

In the early days of the epidemic about fifty girls fell sick. The hospitals were quickly overcrowded and the Nazis issued a ban forbidding further cases from being hospitalised. The leaders of our home emptied a few rooms and converted them into sick-rooms. Whoever could, helped. But all that could be offered was devotion and patience, kindness and conscientiousness, as there were few or no medical supplies.

As the epidemic spread, panic and fear grew, but Mrs Rósa and the other carers managed to contain it. They spent weeks on their feet, day and night. Typhoid carries with it an enormous amount of waste and filth, and I am still puzzled about how those tired-out yet compassionate people coped. They had to fight our shattered mental state and confront our anguish when friends were dying before our eyes. During just the first few days of the epidemic twelve girls died. Mrs Rósa was an extraordinary mother to us, even in those initial days when she had to fight for the life of her own daughter Rája.

Here is a poem written during the epidemic by a *Mädchenheim* girl, twelve-year-old Eva Picková.

Fear

Today the ghetto knows a different fear.
Close in its grip, Death wields an icy scythe.
An evil sickness spreads terror in its wake,
The victims of its shadow weep and writhe.

Today a father's heartbeat tells his fright
And mothers bow their heads into their hands.
Now children choke and die with typhoid here
A bitter toll is taken from their ranks.

My heart still beats inside my breast
While friends depart for other worlds.
Perhaps it's better – who can say? –
Than watching this, to die today?

No, no, my God, we want to live,
Not watch our numbers melt away!
We want to have a better world,
We want to work – we must not die!

Eva was to be murdered in Auschwitz on 18 December of that same year.

Meanwhile, Rája Engländerová, who had turned fourteen since writing the census description that I have quoted, wrote her own essay about her illness. It was called 'How my father saved my life'.

It is 1943. A typhoid epidemic has seized the Terezín ghetto and it has spread disastrously. In our room of twenty-five, a few girls have become ill. After a while, I also contracted typhoid. I am fourteen years old. I was put into isolation. My ward had been a store room, a dark place with an arched ceiling and closed external shutters, where day and night only a bare globe shone. Being here was cause enough for despair. Fifty ill people lived, suffered, and were dying here. Children, and young and old women, constantly refilled the vacant beds. Whenever anyone died, their still-warm bed was taken by a new patient. There was no medication, not enough nurses and no one who could even give you water. It only remained to wait for death. In isolation.

For three weeks I had a fever. My body weakened. All those familiar dreams returned again and again in my burning head. The will to live was all but extinguished and there was nobody to revive it. Each person fought her battle alone. The surroundings, which I registered in flashes of awareness, were ghastly and it was better to slip into semi-consciousness and drift into nothingness.

At the moment when life was slipping away from me, the nurse brought me a letter which still smelt of disinfectant. It was from my father. With the last bit of willpower, I forced myself to read it. I looked at the numbers and mathematical formulas uncomprehendingly and tried to understand the letter. Father wrote:

'I think that you have been idle long enough. I expect you are getting better. It's time for you to return to your studies so that you don't forget everything. I am sending you a few problems. Work them out and send them back. I'll correct them and send you more.'

Not wanting to hurt Father, I exerted my last ounce of strength and concentrated on solving a few simple problems. Completely exhausted, I handed the folded piece of paper to the nurse to send. Two days later another letter arrived with the corrected work and a few new exercises. I had begun to enjoy them. Slowly, I started to

*emerge from my world of dreams and I began the painful journey
back to life. From time to time moments of despair overtook me,
but life regained its hold and I refused to die.*

*As weak as a newborn creature and reduced to skin and bone, I
learned to walk again. The day came when I tottered towards the
visitors' window and behind the glass stood my father. We looked
at each other in silence. Then tears began to stream down my
face.*

*'Why are you crying?' His voice was trying to be firm. 'Your
maths is getting better, although it was hard work.'*

In 1945, after the liberation, Rája Engländerová returned to Prague.

As soon as the home had more or less recovered from the horrors
of the typhoid epidemic, another disaster occurred. More transports. Again! In the days following the departure of a transport
(each containing about 1,000 people), quarters and bunks around
us were empty. We walked around like phantoms. The sense of loss
and sadness was terrible. Once again, only the discipline of our
carers stopped us from drowning in hopeless indifference and
filth. Why take out a broom? What's the point? Is anything
worthwhile?

After each transport, new occupants moved into the vacated
bunks. They were not accepted kindly but often with animosity.
After all, they were taking the places of dear friends. The newcomers were intruders, foreigners. We forgot that it had been the same
with us. But who else could we take out our anger and hurt on?
Even then, Irena and Kamila were always trying to reunite us, to
resuscitate the will to live. On the whole, they succeeded. It was a
difficult task because as soon as things were more or less stable,
more transports were scheduled and this meant new farewells, new
partings. This was the rhythm and law of our ghetto, earning it its
reputation as the mildest concentration camp, as 'only' a transit
station to the east. In reality, Terezín was a waiting-room for the
gas chambers of Auschwitz.

Here is another of the *Mädchenheim* essays. Its writer, S.G.,
was thirteen years old, and lived in room 28.

Rumours are beginning to fly around Terezín that a transport of

5,000 people will leave. There is tension in the streets, in the Homes and in the rooms. Here and there you can hear this kind of conversation:

'I tell you that if this transport leaves, I'll be on it ...'

'Don't say that. After all, you are protected, but I am just a labourer in the Reitschule [riding school].

Unfortunately, they are not rumours as is sometimes the case, but the truth. That night 5,000 people are *summoned to the transport.*

Some of the girls at the Home already knew who would be on it. My best friend was to be among them. I felt that I couldn't be without her, it would be so terrible. I could confide everything to her, now I will have no one. We were all anxious but nothing happened during the night or the next morning and we became so agitated that we couldn't stay inside. At noon still nothing. It was early afternoon when one of us, Chicky, received her summons. But nobody else. We thought she would cry, but our Chicky was brave. It was evening when Pavla was summoned – and my best friend, Olga. Her parents didn't want to tell her. We thought we wouldn't be able to get to sleep but, after a while, we slept.

In the morning, transport slips were distributed to the next batch of people, who were on the reserve list. Our Popi and Helena were included. Everyone had to pack up and assemble at 3 in the afternoon. Nobody could imagine the horrors which would emerge during the afternoon ...

Chicky's father came over, wanting to help her pack. Chicky offered him three tomatoes which she had secretly brought in from the fields but he said no: 'Keep them, Zdenička, I am so hungry that I'd eat the lot.' Then he began to cry and it was clear that he had not eaten and that the whole family had nothing, not even a piece of bread. When we heard that, we cried too and we all searched for food. For the third time I had seen a man cry. Zdenka kissed us joyfully because her small suitcase was now full of food but we said, 'Don't forget that we are one family and that's why we help each other ... and anyway, it's customary!'

Olga had nothing suitable to wear so we gave her whatever we could. They left at 3 p.m.

That night in bed it felt strange because some girls were absent. Oh yes, they had gone. Later on we said, 'It will never be the same room again.'

Our sense of self-preservation had weakened. It seemed that the desire to abandon life was overpowering, and we began courting voluntary inclusion on a transport with a departing friend, sweetheart or parents. Often, seemingly by chance, we bustled about on the ramp, a danger zone during the boarding of a transport. Sometimes someone would deliberately bump into a guard in order to be caught and squeezed into the cattle car now, not later. Why stay any longer? What is there to wait for? Ironically, fate played games with us. Often the opposite thing happened: those who protected themselves perished while others, who risked death, survived.

I remember my friend Franta Stránský, a medical student and a wonderful baritone. He had sung in *The Bartered Bride* and *The Kiss*. When he was summoned to the transport, he injected himself in the leg with a substance which caused a really high temperature (as he wished) and normally this would have ensured his exclusion. This time, however, everybody, including those who were seriously ill, had to leave on the transport. The Germans had altered their tactics and Franta paid for it. It is unlikely that he was alive when the cattle wagons with their human cargo arrived at Auschwitz.

After several days of enduring this and similar departures, we changed. We were subdued and miserable – and we aged. We constantly went through emotional highs and lows at the *Mädchenheim*. It was the carers who made sure that life would go on as usual. In daily administrative meetings, our individual problems were tackled, probably in the same way as the problem of providing paper for our studies. The German authorities strictly forbade teaching. Even though the plan for 'the final solution of the Jewish question' was being implemented, what would happen if some of the Jews survived? The Germans did not want the Jews to be educated.

The SS guards loathed to walk through the quarters of Terezín. These 'rulers of the world' feared sickness as the devil fears the cross. But, in spite of that, raiding squads occasionally invaded both the girls' and boys' homes and turned everything upside down. They looked for evidence – text books, exercise books, drawings. But our hiding places for paper, pencils and books were very good. The SS suspected that we kept on studying, but they never found anything. There was an anonymous poem written in *Mädchenheim*, called 'Pain burns me, the pain of Terezín'.

Fifteen beds, fifteen charts with names,
Fifteen people without a family tree,
Fifteen bodies tortured by medicine and pills
Beds over which the crimson blood of ages spills.
Fifteen bodies that want to live here.
Thirty eyes seeking quietness.
Bald heads which gape out of the prison.
The holiness of the suffering, what's that to me?

The loveliness of air, which day after day
Smells of strangeness and carbolic.
The nurses who carry thermometers,
Mothers who seek a smile.
Food is such a luxury here.
Long, long nights and short days.

Yet I don't want to leave this place
Of sunny rooms and burning cheeks.
Nurses drifting, only a shadow of help
For little sufferers.

I would like to stay here, a sick little one
Where the doctor visits daily.
Until, after a long time, I would be well again.

Then, I would like to live
And return home again.

The arrival of a transport (drawing by Leo Haas).

Bread carried in a hearse – the major form of transportation in Terezín (drawing by Malvina Schalkoá).

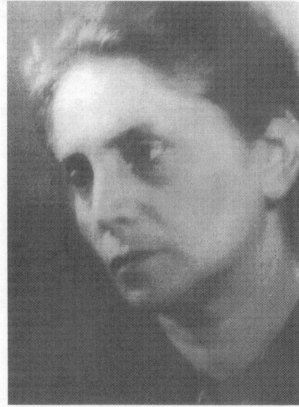

Above
The Terezín
Square. To the
right of the
church is the
Mädchenheim.
Right
Rósa
Engländerová,
our carer, in
1941.

*Grandfather's card to me **(above)** and my official acknowledgement for the parcels **(below)**.*

May 1945. 'I have empty hands, there is no one anywhere, nothing remains.'

*The 'census',
17 November
1943 (drawing
by Leo Haas).*

Drückt man auf dem einen Ende mit 1 kg auf $\frac{1}{10}$ cm^2 und ist das andere 50 cm^2 dann erhält man einen Druck: $\frac{50}{10} + 1 \, kg = 5 \, kg$

Anwendung: Hydraulische Presse.
Ist das Verhältnis der Flächen z. B. 1 : 100
d. h. die Fläche des Presskolbens ist 100 mal größer als die Fläche des Druckkolbens, dann ist der erzielte Druck 100 mal so groß.

Beispiel: Der Durchmesser des Druckkolbens = 5 cm
Der Durchmesser " Press " = 100 cm

Wie groß ist die Kraft P mit der ich drücken muß damit der Körper bei E mit 2000 kg gedrückt wird?

Zuerst muß man die Flächen berechnen. Die Fläche eines Kreises

A: Durchmesser x Durchmesser x pi dividiert durch 4. oder

kurz: $F = \frac{d^2 \pi}{4}$

Die Fläche des Druckkolbens ist $\frac{5 \times 5 \times 3.14}{4} = 19.6 \, cm^2$

Die Fläche des Presskolbens $\frac{100 \times 100}{4} \cdot 3.14 = 7900 \, cm^2$

Das Verhältnis der Flächen ist $\frac{7900}{19.6} = 400$

Der Presskolben drückt mit der 400 fachen Kraft wie der Druckkolben. Wenn ich mit 2000 kg am Presskolben drücken will, dann brauche ich am Druckkolben den 400 sten Teil oder

$\frac{2000}{400} = 50 \, kg.$

Es genügt also 50 kg am Druckkolben um 2000 kg am Presskolben zu bekommen.

Rája Engländerová's letter from her father during typhoid.

Above
A poster for the Freizeitgestaltung
(Leisure activities), signed by
Hedda Grábová.
Right
The conductor Rafael
Schächter (drawing by Petr Kien).

G.VERDI:

REQUIEM

DIRIGENT: RAFAEL SCHÄCHTER

SOLI:

G. BORGER   SOPRAN
H. ARANSON LINDT   MEZZO-SOPRAN
D. GRÜNFELD   TENOR
K. BERMANN   BASS

GEMISCHTER CHOR

AM KLAVIER: GIDEON KLEIN

Left
Verdi's Requiem *in Terezín.*
Below
The 'café' (drawing by Leo Haas).

Dancing on the edge of death

The attic of the former Terezín brewery was unbelievably spacious. Twice or three times weekly I visited Father there instead of going straight to the *Mädchenheim* from work. Directly under the roof, there were tiny, ingeniously constructed cells made of masonite and hessian. Each had its own door. The cells, in which lived two, only two men, created an illusion, an expression of the deep human longing for privacy and home. Above each bed it was possible to pin pictures or photos on the wall. The luckiest occupants had even received their own padlock and could secure their privacy with a key. These tiny rooms were about two and a half by three metres but, compared with the barracks dormitories, with their three layers of bunks and hundreds of people, they were a miracle. Only men who worked lived in this attic and my father was one of these.

He was fifteen years older than my mother, but always looked younger than his age. He was a very handsome man. In fact, when I was five, he was the first man I wanted to marry. Now he looked old, older than he was. Until quite recently, he had been in the carpenters' gang which even worked outside the ghetto walls. The carpenters lived in the Sudeten Barracks. Father was lucky as they were excellent fellows: Karel Švenk (cabaret singer, composer, actor and director all in one), Franta Goldscheider, the conductor Rafael Schächter and others. They came to Terezín with some artistic background and, right from the start, even here, they tried to use their talents. At first it was for their own pleasure, but later it was for the other inmates too. These young men, so full of optimism, used to call my father 'Papa', and he felt comfortable among them.

And Mother? Even here she was a very pretty and attractive woman – I, her own daughter, knew it. I knew also that my relationship with her was complicated. Again it was because of Father. He loved her tenderly and passionately, as his tiny, elegant, intelligent and charming wife, but also as his baby, his little girl. He called her 'my *medlička'*. His Czech had a smattering of German and this nickname was coined from the word *mädchen* (girl).

Mother had always had a circle of admirers and in Terezín it was the same. I don't know how and where she first met Professor M., formerly a professor at Berlin University and now a member of the *Ältestenrat*, but he helped Father find a sought-after position in the Terezín bakery. Many younger men waited for just such a job. Father received an extra quarter of a loaf of bread a day. That quarter loaf represented a valuable token of exchange – for cigarettes, for an English check blanket, left by someone who had died, from which a skirt and jacket could be made (even in the ghetto it was possible to be fashionable), and many other things. But the quarter loaf also meant sleepless nights next to the hot oven, instead of restful sleep. It meant a twisted and sore back from working an eleven-hour shift carrying long planks holding rows of grey, heavy loaves of raw dough or baked brown bread.

The sun had shone on Father, the carpenter, while he worked with the scented wood; they say he even sang (out of tune!) with his fellow workers. The oven heat scorched Father, the baker, while his nostrils got blocked with grey, sticky flour and his pallor deepened to the flour's colour. Father visibly deteriorated, but he could not refuse this prized job. I was angry, very angry, with my mother. I was also angry with myself. I was nearly an adult. I was sixteen, and I was such a coward that I was unable to speak to Mother and compel her to see Father the way I did.

I visited Father in the brewery attic as often as I could. In winter, it was so cold that there could have been an ice rink there, but in August,

Father's last August, it was terribly hot. There were throat-irritating layers of dust everywhere and I passed one door after another made of roughly sawn timber. There was no one about (most of the men were still working) and in unnatural, almost scary, silence I stumbled in the dark over the beams to Father's door, number 117. The padlock was not in its bolt, so Father was there, but perhaps he was sleeping? It was Sunday and I had a small gift for him, a little bowl I had carved from some pine bark I found. I was checked by the silence. It was somehow different. And then I heard what was like suppressed, fast breathing. Moaning? It raced through my mind that Father was suffering or even dying. The sweat trickled down my back. My gasping throat uttered, 'Father, Father, what's the matter? Open the door, please!'

After a while, Father said unexpectedly and in a very strange voice, 'Wait a bit.'

I wanted to run away, but as I was obedient I waited. I moved back a few steps to a spot where the attic window let in a little light. Here, there was a run-down harmonium on which, only a few days before, a man who was infatuated with me had sung and played a Negro spiritual. In this town, or rather in this place where my father's bread was carried on hearses dragged by human beings, a run-down harmonium in a brewery attic seemed quite normal.

All at once, door no. 117 opened and a stream of hazy light struck the passage. Still behind the door, rapidly and with embarrassment, I began to babble something about how, not so long ago, I had played 'The Blue Danube' on the piano at home for Father's pleasure.

'Father, would you like me to play on this hoot of a harmonium for you? I might be able to,' I babbled tremulously. Suddenly I realised that Father was not alone. He was paler than his bread dough and was standing uneasily looking at Mother, his hands shaking. They were scurrying around the unmade bed, Father straightening the pillow and Mother the blanket. I looked at Father's hands. We were so alike, even our hands, but mine, then, had no liver spots.

Mother was on the verge of leaving, secure and unembarrassed. She said nothing. What was there to say, why should she apologise? There was no reason. But I, yes, I had butted into their precious intimacy and should apologise. Mother never apologised for anything; she was always firmly convinced that she behaved correctly and that it was up to her to decide what to do or not do. It often surprised me that everybody, including Father, believed her. On this occasion, as always, she left just when things could be uncomfortable for her. Often in my own life I envied this skill of Mother's.

In my thoughts, I begged her to stay, not to leave me alone with Father, lest I should hate her. Above all, I wanted to love her as unconditionally as her husband, my father, did, if only she would not leave. I would not be able to fill the emptiness which her departure created. And already I could hear Father asking her to stay, insisting that the three of us would be all right. Father looked so grey and miserable that my heart was breaking. I was the adult, while his 'child', his *medlička*, sweetly disappeared. At sixteen, I could not unreservedly share Father's unconditional love for Mother, and in that limited living space it was not possible to pretend. I was just about to open my mouth and say what I knew at the time about Mother and Professor M. To this day I am grateful that something restrained me. I realised, like an adult, that Father saw his wife the way he wanted to, that he could not live without her and the wonderful light-hearted atmosphere she created. For him my mother was unique, irreplaceable. I knew and still know that he also loved me very much.

I kept quiet and sat on the edge of the re-made bed, even though I wanted to cry out, destroy the framework of lies (which was how, in my immaturity, I saw it). Why didn't I ask you, Father, where is your wife going now, where was she yesterday when you were earning that damned crust of bread, and who procured that bakery-hell job for you? Do you know that for a few weeks I have been observing her, and I vacillate between the wish to know the truth and the desire to know nothing, to maintain illusions about your perfect wife and her love, about your perfect marriage? That is why, in the past few weeks, I haven't been able to look you in the eye. And you complained to Mother about me, about how unpleasant I am and without feelings. Then you told me that you would kill me if I were like the other girls, about whom the boys at the bakery speak so disrespectfully. You were almost nasty to me, but I know that this was from love and anxiety because you know that you cannot protect me, and because you know that my behaviour depends entirely on myself. If nothing else, however, you offer me an example of moral strength ...

Later, I would be deeply glad that I had found the strength to keep quiet. At the time, that sort of truth would have been out of place. A few weeks later, my father was picked for the transport to Auschwitz and he left me and, worst of all, his *medlička,* for ever.

Envisaging nothing of that, on that boiling hot August afternoon, I was swept by a wave of sadness: a while ago, I recalled, before Terezín, things had not seemed right at home. It was during my last half-year holiday, when I could still attend school. Our cosy apartment had smelt of after-Christmas incense. Our American-made heater radiated comfort, the burning coke glowed. In the evening twilight, knees under my chin, I sat close to the fire and sinking into the armchair I almost purred with contentment.

The dark, friendly quiet was suddenly broken by two voices, male and female. Both voices, intimate and gentle, sounded sure of their aloneness. I knew the man's voice. It was our family friend, Major N. Now, his voice was caressing and not as sharp as it had been a few weeks ago in the street, when we were out together and a private soldier failed to notice and salute the major. The other voice, Mother's, was more cautious. Even then, she was applying the dictum she would teach me after the war as I grew into adulthood: 'Always be loved more; like, but don't love.' Yet in spite of this, Mother's voice was quite special now, speaking in a different tone from that of our Sunday meals around the table.

I jumped up quickly and feverishly turned on the light. The two of them stood very close to each other and Mother smiled sweetly at me. Everything seemed the same as usual and I was almost embarrassed by my suspicious thoughts.

All this came back to my mind in Father's small, overheated cell. I kept quiet. What is truth and what are lies? Lies which help you to survive ... So, Father, I told you nothing.

Father reached into the pocket of his baker's coat which was hanging on a hook, and pulled out a quarter of a loaf of fresh bread. Without a word, he gave me the bread, and this was the only thing that made any sense. He was so close, yet so far. How I wanted to hold him and rock him, as if he were my own child! Carefully, with my palm, I claimed Mother's hairpin which had been left lying on the blanket. I knew I should stay, but I couldn't. The handleless door did not even squeak, so my departure was hardly noticed. Only the attic boards creaked with my every step and I gripped the bread so tightly that my thumb made a hole in it.

'I saw a picture in the Slavonic Bible of A.D. 863. The Antichrist is going to spear a saint, but the saint sits composedly as though it does not concern him. I used to think that artists of the Middle Ages could not paint emotions such as fear, surprise, pain and so on, because it appears as if their saints are unconcerned about being tortured. Now I know better: what else could they do?'

The speaker was the Czech journalist and author Karel Poláček, in a lecture he gave in Terezín shortly before being gassed in Auschwitz.

Yes. Perhaps saints of the Middle Ages passively accepted torture because 'God's will is good will'. But we in the Terezín ghetto, in the twentieth century, witnessed an entirely different and remarkable process. It is difficult to describe, let alone evaluate. In the whole history of mankind it would be hard to find a similar situation, in which people on the edge of an abyss, on the brink of death, created works of art, composed music, produced operas, sang their own requiems.

In 1935, when Hitler announced the Nuremberg Laws, he was legalising the means for persecution of the Jews who had been moving throughout Europe for a thousand years before. Jews were targeted as 'internal enemies of the Reich' and as an inferior race against whom any actions were permitted. Elsewhere in Europe, life went on normally. Even before the occupation of Czechoslovakia, however, some artists of Jewish origin began using pseudonyms.

After the occupation by the Nazis in 1939, the conditions worsened day by day for everyone, but especially for the Jews. In 1941, there came a new law which stipulated that all musical instruments owned by Jews had to be surrendered. So music was then only performed privately in people's homes, and at great risk. Yet the number and quality of chamber music evenings in Jewish homes was significant and possibly influenced later musical activity in concentration camps, particularly Terezín.

The first transports from Prague to Terezín in 1941 included many musicians. Among them were Gideon Klein, Rafael Schächter, Karel Švenk, the composer Pavel Haas, Carlo and Erica Taube, Hedda Grabová and the violinist Egon Ledeč who had been concertmaster of the Czech Philharmonic. It quickly emerged that music could play a significant role in maintaining continuity between the life left behind and the current detention, and that music could expand the capacity to defy hopelessness. From the beginning of the ghetto's existence, music was heard in the living-quarters, in attics, cellars and courtyards.

For quite a long time people sang and played illegally. It was dangerous but they took the risk.

Then in 1942, the Nazis decided to turn Terezín into a 'model' camp (*Musterlager*) – a public relations gesture to the International Red Cross and to the world at large. The Jewish Council, therefore, became able to obtain permission for cultural activities. The artists were even allowed to set up an independent action group – *Freizeitgestaltung* (leisure activities) – in which artists such as Gideon Klein, Rafael Schächter and Paul Libenský were involved.

Initially, musical instruments had been smuggled into Terezín by the first prisoners in their 50-kilogram allowance of luggage. If possible, instruments had been dismantled so that they could be slipped in through the checkpoints. Some people had also brought sheet music, opera scores and books. These people chose kilograms of cultural, rather than practical, items. Apart from instruments and music, it was possible to find Goethe's *Faust* or the poetry of Rimbaud. With the instruments, paints, brushes, and books, inmates carried an awareness of their own capacity, an awareness of their past and their responsibility to it. It became evident that intrinsic human creativity can endure under any circumstances. For those few who were to survive, it became apparent that even the most horrifying situations can sometimes strengthen people and liberate qualities of which they themselves were not aware.

The first, and most easily accessible, instrument was the human voice. Even in the beginning, when men and women were completely segregated, choirs were formed in the various barracks. The first choir was a liturgical one led by Cantor Fischer from Teplice. The choir sang psalms. By 6 December 1941, the men from the Sudeten Barracks had prepared an 'evening of miscellany' in which an accordion accompanied violin and flute solos. That evening consolidated an emerging musical tradition.

Just a fortnight before this, transport AK1 had arrived at Terezín. It consisted of young, sturdy, men who had left Prague allegedly to work. Indeed there was work but not what they expected. Even before the train had left Prague it was clear that they had been duped. On the evening of their arrival, they appeared in the barracks and received their orders: to prepare Terezín for the influx of thousands of Jews. In the three dormitories of the Sudeten Barracks there were about 120 young men. Surprisingly, they were neither overwhelmingly sad nor sceptical – the end of the war seemed on the horizon! Hope always renews the desire to live. In the dark winter evenings these young men met in one of the dormitories and passed the time by exchanging jokes, telling stories and singing songs. Alexandr Singer was in this group. A week later, Rafael Schächter, who was to become such a significant figure in Terezín's musical world, was one of its members.

I am glad that many years ago, before Alexandr Singer, his wife and three children emigrated from Czechoslovakia, I recorded his narrative.

'On 24 November 1941, as instructed, I arrived at Prague's railway station. Young Jewish men had been conscripted to work, but it did not seem so bad because we had been told that after a week we would return home. Even before the train departed, we realised it was a trap. I became inmate number 284. That same day I arrived in Terezín. There were three dormitories for 120 men who were supposed to prepare for the arrival of the next transports. There were no straw mattresses or blankets in the Sudeten Barracks.

'From the beginning, at evening gatherings, we helped each other forget depressing thoughts. We encouraged each other and everyone who knew a joke or could sing entertained the others without being prompted. That's how the first "cabarets" began. About this time Karel Švenk appeared. I knew Švenk from Prague where we had sung together in Švenk's Club of Lost Talent. Švenk also directed and acted at the club with Jiří Süssland.

'After work, when we met in the barracks, Švenk gradually influenced the impromptu performances and, without anyone noticing, the first program was born. I sang Ukrainian, Russian and Slovakian folk songs. I sang in a rather high, distinctive, falsetto tenor, to an increasingly large audience. I had a natural sense of music.

'After AK1, other transports followed. Those on Transport H arrived at the Sudeten Barracks on 30 November 1941 and Rafael Schächter was among them. On the first night the "old settlers" discovered Schächter's short temper and captivating personality. He barged into a room where the daily, improvised cabaret took place and announced that there were excellent singers there. He pounced on me, a stranger to him until now, and confessed that his passion was music. He immediately invited those interested to perform ("let's say Czech folk songs") as a choir. He did not ask if there were any obstacles. The choir simply had to be.

'In the days that followed, the men were sent to different work-shops. Rafael did clerical work for the bag-makers. It had its advantages. One was a pass allowing movement between the Sudeten and Hamburg Barracks, and hence greater opportunities to organise things. Rafael immediately asked if I could also work with the bag-makers. He wanted me with him. He decided that we would study music together and he would teach me singing. He said that he could not leave such a voice idle. He wanted, as much as possible, to pro-vide me with music school training. I was overjoyed. I was young, eager, and now not only was I able to leave the barracks but I could dedicate myself to music.

'Rafael was as tenacious as a young bulldog. There were no barri-ers that he could not overcome. In no time at all the first mixed choir was formed. It learnt about five Czech and Moravian songs. My first solo performance, which had been prepared by Rafael, was a song with the choir: "The horses are being led out for me". The audience's reaction, in the courtyard of the Cavalier Barracks, indicated the power of art, especially music, for people who had been driven from their homes and stripped of their basic human rights.

'Soon after that initial performance Professor Ausspitz, an outstand-ing music teacher, arrived on the first transport from Brno. His students had included Leo Slezák, Richard Tauber and others. The 78-year-old teacher heard the "Cavalier" choir in the courtyard. That day he ap-proached me and declared firmly, "You must study, young man. I will take it upon myself. Look here, this is how to sing from the middle register to high C" – and the old man brilliantly executed the scale.

'So a second teacher had joined Rafael. I continued working with the bag-makers and, at the same time, studied with Schächter, who had his own private objective: to use, as soon as possible, the Czech and international opera scores which he had brought into Terezín. Rafael Schächter, "Rafík", then began preparing me for the role of Jeník in Smetana's *Bartered Bride*. Initially, only individual arias. The first Mařenka with whom I sang was played by a delightful girl with long, blonde hair. I can see her in front of me, alive and sweet, but I have forgotten her name.

'Every one is inside me, every one of those with whom I shared months of sheer pleasure, both those who did not come one day be-cause they had left on transports and others who took their places.

'Perhaps these recollections are the only headstones that one can erect. I must especially mention one who, at that time, moved about dejectedly only to subsequently disappear and never return. The famous concert singer Grünfeld had come on the Prague transport. Rafík and I took him into our company immediately. We wanted him to sing with us and help dispel the haunting sadness in his eyes. We did not succeed. He was so unhappy, so disappointed in people, that he had no desire to sing or even to live. He could not reconcile himself to the fact that the people who had caused this revival of the Dark Ages, complete with torture and inquisitions, were members of a nation whose famous songs he had so recently sung all over Europe. He wanted to leave for the east on a transport, he sought death and it found him soon enough. Although Schächter did what he could to secure Grünfeld's release from the transport, he was not successful. The Nazis knew him only too well from the Berlin and Leipzig opera companies. He accepted the slip of paper with its summons to the transport quietly, passively, almost thankfully. He left forever.

'In 1942 the other Grünfeld arrived – David. He was also an outstanding singer. His Italian training (he had studied with Carpi in Prague) had eradicated any harshness in his voice and endowed it with a magical lightness and strong expression. Rafík now decided to rehearse a whole opera. Grünfeld's start in Terezín was demanding. He laboured hard and, after work, he sang. He even learnt several roles at once. He sang not only with Schächter, but with Egon Klein, the Viennese conductor, and with the famous Viennese soprano Madame Hecht. In Vienna she was renowned as the Queen of the Night in Mozart's *Magic Flute*. Because of this, Klein rehearsed a concert performance of that opera. At this time everybody believed, we must have believed, that we would live to see the end of the war. David Grünfeld actually did. In May 1945 he returned to Terezín in a death march from Auschwitz, ill, and without his family. It was a wretched return.

'Later, unbearable memories drove him to emigrate to the U.S.A. He sang with the New York City Opera Company and was later engaged in West Germany as a permanent member of the Wiesbaden Opera. The repertoire of Czech operas which he had sung in Terezín with Rafael Schächter was fully utilised there. In West Germany he was known as David Garen. He died in 1962, aged only forty-six. The war had finally struck him down.

'In the original cast for the Terezín *Bartered Bride*, David Grünfeld was supposed to sing Vašek. But as he was not Czech – he was from

Užhorod (Ungvár–Ruthenia) – he had difficulty coping with Vašek's stammering part. In any case, David's melancholy nature did not suit Vašek's comic style. Even for a concert performance, Rafík was not only particular about musical ability but also acting ability. So a change in the cast took place – Grünfeld was Jeník and I was Vašek. Karel Berman, a soloist from the National Opera Theatre in Prague, joined the cast as the indispensable Kecal, and a charming woman, the mature and beautiful Podolierová, was Mařenka. Schächter patiently taught her the Czech text and she managed it excellently, even though her mother tongue was German. Among the soloists were František Stránský and Windholz, a professional singer of German origin. Those who did not believe that an emotionally and physically abused group of people could sing "Let's rejoice, let's be merry", the opening chorus of The Bartered Bride, listened with tears in their eyes. They listened with joy to a miracle. More than ever before, they realised what it meant to be a human being.

'Rafael Schächter was extremely versatile. As well as presenting the Czech repertoire, including another Smetana opera The Kiss, he loved Verdi and Mozart and directed The Marriage of Figaro in German. He was strict. He could walk around all day with shoelaces undone and not even notice, but he did not overlook one wrong note, or a single rest. "A rest is also music" was his favourite saying. Sometimes, when discussing things with a friend on a nearby bunk, he would debate in such a vigorous way that he scattered items of clothing around the whole room. His absent-mindedness disappeared, however, as soon as he sat at the piano or the harmonium. He concentrated totally, almost physically – that was Rafík. All these qualities came to the fore when he was rehearsing a particularly demanding work such as Verdi's Requiem. There was not a single person in his choir, nor a soloist, who was not as passionately absorbed in the greatness of music as Rafael Schächter.

'Yet little things revealed the depth of his humanity. Behind his fiery bohemian artist's soul, a child's joyful sense of humour, gentleness and playfulness often lurked. Rafík had high standards when he held auditions for the choir. Considering the conditions under which he and "his" people had to work, it was almost farcical. The choir was constantly falling apart, and he had to keep finding new choristers – untrained singers – when choir members (and soloists) left, never to return. In spite of this, his demands never diminished.

'At half past five in the morning, before work, Rafík would come and wake me up. "Get up," he would say as he shook me, "a person can only learn properly in the early morning! If you want to perform Vašek's arias from *The Bartered Bride* rhythmically, you must practise now!" 'When he believed that his opinion was right, he was uncompromising. The well-known Prague singer Hedda Grábová-Kernmayrová was among the soloists. After Professor Ausspitz's death, she took over teaching me. Once, Rafík listened for quite a while behind the door when I was having a lesson. Suddenly, he burst in and exclaimed, "You will not teach him." He said nothing more. He did not approve of a singer practising scales and "shouting". Schächter understood the teaching of voice and was convinced that "to sing *forte* is not art".

'Schächter was a conductor, a répétiteur, the orchestra's representative; he was a music teacher and a friend of those with whom he worked. Months of intensive work in such a bizarre environment were as valuable as years and fostered new, and until then unknown, kinships. Friendships which would never have blossomed in a lifetime of freedom were forged in a matter of hours, let alone weeks or months, by sharing a common interest – music. Music was a substitute for personal relationships, community culture and national tradition. It dispelled hunger and sadness, it embraced knowledge. Perhaps this was so because its practitioners danced on the edge of death.

'The last rehearsal that I attended was Verdi's *Requiem* in the gymnasium. It was the final rehearsal. For several days there had been whispers in the ghetto about more transports but, as always, nothing definite was known about when it would go, or how many it would take. People spoke of labour camps etc. The rehearsal proceeded in an atmosphere of apprehension about the future, the fear that a husband, a wife or a child would be "chosen". Rafík did not reveal that he was aware of their tight throats: he was as demanding as ever and, during the course of several hours, actually succeeded in helping everyone forget the present. The *Dies Irae* was powerful and unrestrained.

'In the afternoon I received my call-up slip of paper for the transport. Rafík, from whom I parted, was as sure as the others that it was a work transport for "somewhere near Leipzig". He implored me that, on arrival, I would immediately form a choir so that when he himself came, we could continue working. He was convinced that we would continue together. How fortunate it was that he did not know that the transport was neither a work transport, nor went to Leipzig, but to the death ramps of Auschwitz.

'I left on 28 September 1944. Then more transports left, one after the other. Some of the musicians met on this final journey, others never came across each other again. On 16 October, Rafael Schächter left as well. What is left to say? How wonderful it was that Rafík believed that I was somewhere far away organising singers for his future choir. It was certainly good that he could not imagine that final stage where the concluding act of a person's life is performed. For myself, and for the majority of those who never returned, I, Alexandr Singer, have revealed the most important aspect of my life and the life of my friends.'

The hours and hours which I spent, incredibly happily, in the *Mädchenheim* cellar, or in the back row of the choir during performances of *The Bartered Bride*, *The Kiss* and, most especially, Verdi's *Requiem*, were the most profound experiences of my life and cannot be compared with anything that happened later.

Of the essays which Zdenka Müllerová, the carer in our room, set us to write, I brought back only one. Its topic was: 'My strongest and most positive experience in the Home'.

Room no. 15. Renée Friesová, 16 years old.

We girls in the Mädchenheim *are lucky. Our building, L 410, was the former army headquarters and is very large with extensive cellars. Probably that's why the musicians chose it as the place where they could rehearse concerts and operas. As soon as I moved here, I discovered that I could just go down the stairs to the cellar and suddenly I would find myself part of an incredible fairy tale – a world of exceptional and inspired people in a world of the most beautiful sounds. I do not know how the harmonium appeared there. I only know that Rafael Schächter, conductor, répétiteur and director all in one, could play it as if he were the whole orchestra.*

In spite of working long days in the field, sometimes for eleven hours, I have almost never missed the chance (when there wasn't a lecture) to descend the gloomy stairs to that vaulted, damp room. Rafík would already be seated at the harmonium. He asked me to call him Rafík. All the singers called him that. Two little windows below street level were blocked with bags of straw and covered over with black rags. The singers who were rehearsing for the opera lived elsewhere, but they were allowed to exceed curfew time and had their own passes. Sometimes they rehearsed until midnight.

For a few weeks I sat somewhere in a corner and, hardly breathing, listened to the most exquisitely sung arias in the world. One day Rafík noticed me. 'What are you doing here so often when you don't sing with us? Come and try!'

My legs buckled. I had loved to sing at home but I liked listening more, when Grandpa sang either 'Oh son, my son' or arias from Lohengrin. *Grandpa was a wonderful singer, but I? My singing wasn't worth anything. Much to my surprise, the most magnificent thing in the world happened. Rafík invited me to join the choir. I cannot delude myself. I know he always lacked singers as they were constantly departing on transports, but he also liked me and so he made a pact with me – if there were ever the risk that I might ruin something in a very quiet passage, he would give me a signal and I would only move my lips and not make a sound.*

Once he said of me to either Karel Berman or Šany (Alexandr), 'After all, I can allow myself the luxury of having such a talisman!' Karel Berman, Šany Singer and Franta Stránský are my friends. Perhaps I am attractive to them as a young woman, but I don't see myself as such. I simply admire them all. When Karel Berman sings Negro spirituals to me in his velvety voice, or arias from Blodek's opera In the Well *while playing the harmonium, I have the feeling that I am a queen and that I could experience nothing more beautiful. These are the finest moments I have had in the* Mädchenheim.

When I was re-reading my little essay, after more than fifty years, a funny incident sprang to mind. At the time, however, it did not seem comical at all.

There was a young woman who sang in Rafael Schächter's choir who appeared to me to be very sophisticated. I heard that she had been brought up in a convent. I didn't really know Nina well. Remote and severe, she was Terezín-thin, with long, blonde hair done up in a bun. She was not particularly beautiful but her voice certainly was. I do not know whether she was patronising to everybody, but she was to me. Nina, with her clear, well-trained soprano voice, was one of the strengths of Rafík's choir. I was not. Indeed, I was there more as a good luck charm, as he used to say. Nor was I slender like Nina. I was one of those people who, perhaps because of a hormonal irregularity, was plump. To eat the inadequate Terezín food and still look good made me feel guilty.

Nina spoke to me only once. She came up to me one evening during a rehearsal and, in front of other people, said a single sentence: 'What a waste, such a face with such a body.'

I do not know if the snub was calculated or spontaneous, but she wounded me to the quick. Until then, I had never had a complex about my looks, as boys liked me.

As I stood there, mute, someone said, 'Look, Nina, leave her alone. You are madly in love with Karel Berman, and he stares at Renée more than at you. You're jealous, aren't you?'

That someone had stood up to her made amends, but only partly.

As I have mentioned before, houses in the fortress of Terezín formed regular, geometrical blocks. Originally, the individual houses had been separated, one from the other, by walls, but when Terezín became a ghetto, the walls between the houses were haphazardly knocked down. On whose orders, or why, I do not know. I do know, however, that it created links between the houses and yards, and this enabled people to move around even after the curfew. Almost daily in these courtyards, artists sang, acted, performed magic tricks, and read or recited their own poetry or that of world-famous writers. The shows were like cabarets and, like traditional music or the theatre, they offered unhappy people moments of joy and forgetfulness. There were always a lot of performers and large audiences.

As I lived in the *Mädchenheim*, I could not often get out to enjoy the courtyard cabarets. We were not allowed out at night without a pass. For me, however, there was nothing more delightful than our cellar and, in it, Rafael Schächter and his splendid singers. Before lights out we sometimes went to concerts and plays staged in the attics or the rooms set aside for them in the barracks. There was also a café in the square, set up when the Germans wanted to display the ghetto to the International Red Cross as a model camp. Other young people did not go there, so neither did I. But I do know that, for a while, Karel Ančerl, then a pianist and in later years principal conductor of the Czech Philharmonic, played there. So also did Mr Satler, a well-known Prague café violinist. Viennese waltzes, coffee substitute and the illusion of pre-war cafés, all gave the older people the chance to open their sad hearts.

As far as the cabarets were concerned, Karel Švenk was the driving force. But he was not alone: other artists with a zest for participating, such as the theatre director Gustav Schorsch, Ota Schwarz, František Zelenka, Gideon Klein, Jirka Spitz, František Miška, Rauch and many others joined him. There were actors, pianists, producers, narrators and dancers. Visual artists also worked with them, producing scenery or backdrops which complemented Švenk's singing.

I am glad that for a period my father lived in the Sudeten Barracks with these courageous men who, in their own way, managed to overcome their fearfulness. From the age of eleven when both his parents died, Father had had to fend for himself. In spite of being unusually industrious he never became very wealthy, not even as a wine and liquor merchant. He had had little time to acquire an education. He did not have a musical ear, yet he had always loved to hum operetta arias. He now lived and worked with the carpenters and among that group of artists he was quiet, but always an appreciative listener. These talented men liked my father very much and I am grateful to them that, for a while, they were very close to him and gave him some months of relative happiness before he, like most of them, embarked upon his last journey, to Auschwitz.

Behind the ramparts, the prisoners could move from one dormitory to another. It was possible to stage public performances, especially in the uninhabitable attics. These 'theatres' and 'concert halls' differed notably from customary ones: in place of seats there were planks supported by bricks, or beams, or (in the cellars) bare ground and only rarely an old rickety chair. The stage, lighting, props, everything, required imagination. *The Bartered Bride* or *Tosca* might be a concert performance with all performers standing and in Terezín garb, but it still included the choir and soloists. And vocal expression and gestures were more than just 'make believe', they were *real*.

The excitement and pleasure of the actors, singers, musicians and audiences matched the greatest that theatre and music could invoke in people. It was a grand and reciprocal performance. Those on stage gave themselves unstintingly to their audience. As their plight worsened, the audiences for their part increasingly showed their gratitude for a gift which enriched their lives.

I mingled in this environment, which seemed removed from reality, as often as I could. Tickets to concerts and performances cost nothing, but it was difficult to obtain them. The places where they were staged were very small. I tried to see everything, be everywhere and, for example, if Gideon Klein had a concert on any sort of a piano, I was unhappy if I missed it.

Thanks to my father, I knew the group around Karel Švenk. Later, when some of them moved to relatively better conditions than the barracks, I visited them. I recall that Švenk lived in a small room, divided off by hessian, on a kind of balcony in the middle of the ghetto. It was only a stone's throw from the *Mädchenheim* so I used to go there often. That little room was full of papers, props and people. I tried to be invisible, somewhere in a corner, and would closely follow the creation of another cabaret.

At the same time as Švenk's group was enjoying its improvised cabarets in the Sudeten Barracks, something very similar was spontaneously occurring in the women's barracks. A circle of women formed around the singer and actress Hedda Grábová. They began evening performances in darkness or by candlelight (with candles brought from home) as lights were forbidden. As a concertgoer, I heard Hedda Grábová when she sang with Rafael Schächter. There was a newspaper article about her on 29 November 1945, after her return from Terezín, and it was clear from the interview how versatile, widespread and significant the women's activities were.

That little group not only sang and recited for their pleasure, during the long evenings in the dormitories, but later performed in hospitals and gave the patients fresh courage. Hedda Grábová mentioned Švenk's lullaby which the women sang for the sick children:

> My sweet little one, slumber, gently close your eyes,
> The fairies will soon come and bring you a dream.
> All things forbidden in the day will take place in your sleep,
> You shall play in the meadow, little one, where the sun shines.
> You shall gather colourful flowers and smile happily.

There were many other activities which gave us courage and the will to live, but it is impossible for me to recollect them all. There was, however, one heroic gesture by Švenk which only a few witnessed. It was autumn 1944 and the end of the war was within sight.

The Germans were retreating, but even at this late stage they did not lose sight of the fulfilment of their evil goal – the annihilation of the Jewish race. Terezín was a waiting-room for the gas chambers in Poland. It was only now that the cattle wagons took away Karel Švenk, my father, my friends, and more, many more.

The railway track bearing the trains with their endless wagons had been extended to the Hamburg Barracks. Even without having received the call-up slip for a transport, we frequently tried to sneak in there, to spend time with those we loved.

Those summoned to the transport, to 'work', were supposed to take only essential items. Ostensibly, their baggage would be sent after them or brought by their wives or children who were to follow. From a hiding place in the barracks cellar you could see the ramp through a small window and one day what I saw was Karel Švenk, who did not carry a bag. Under his arm he carried a large book. From time to time, when the SS guard was out of sight, he took the book in both hands and as if performing a sacrament he raised it before the eyes of those already in the wagons. The book was Dumas' *Three Musketeers*. It was an old edition and on the cover was a lithograph of 'three men without fear or blemish'. Three invincible men who triumphed on every occasion. What was Švenk trying to say? He just smiled and, surprisingly, he managed to roam around the ramp with his book for quite a while. But his eyes were filled with infinite sadness: they were the eyes of a man who suspected the true purpose of the journey – that it was one for which he needed no baggage at all. Can you understand this incident from *Shoah*, the Holocaust? That, even on a ramp of death, one brave man could inspire others by smiling? This was Švenk's last performance.

Even today I ask this question: what is it in human beings that, on the verge of death, can enable them to laugh, enable them to give and receive joy and happiness? Is it possible that people who know nothing of war and torture, nothing of the cold-blooded murder of millions, can comprehend that in those cruel conditions the victims sometimes sang, smiled and acted? Is it right to tell them? May they not respond, 'They must have been cushy concentration camps, if people could amuse themselves?' Surely such a glib interpretation would detract from the memory of the millions who died? Those millions who perished in the gas chambers, on death marches, or from typhoid and malnutrition? Possibly it would. But the risk of telling what happened is still a risk that is worth taking.

One of the songs Karel Švenk wrote gained the honour of being called the 'Terezín Anthem'. It was not only sung by Czech Jews, but by Jews of other European nationalities.

> Whoever rests on the third level of bunks
> whoever fears dark shadows of the ramparts,
> whoever pleads for a woman's heart in vain
> whoever lives a listless life in the barracks,
> each one, either believing or doubting
> that the sun will warm us once again
> should not despair
> when they hear the anthem played ...
>
> All is possible if you try,
> we'll hold each other's hands,
> despite cruel times, humour is in our hearts,
> day after day we go here and there
> always on the move
> and only thirty words a letter can we dare.
>
> Surely life begins tomorrow,
> and the time approaches
> when we can pack our bundles and head for home.
> All is possible if you try,
> we'll hold each other's hands
> we'll laugh on the ghetto ruins
> then head for home.

Love in a concentration camp

At home, I had been taught that one should use time well as it is irretrievable. I was allowed to read romances and westerns only after the useful tasks had been done. What my grandparents and parents regarded as 'useful' constituted quite a considerable list. Their demands increased, especially after I was forbidden to go to school. I had to learn everything that should have been studied at school and practise the piano two hours daily. Father had a sign hanging above the piano: 'Firkušný practises eight hours daily.' (Rudolf Firkušný was a great Czech-American pianist.) Also, I had to do all the housework, from washing dishes to cleaning windows.

It did not seem to occur to any of the adults that perhaps I would never ever use what I was learning. Father strictly supervised my timetable. Naturally, I slipped away whenever it was possible. Just behind our house were avenues which circled the whole town, and meadows and parks. Josefov, the fortress town where we lived, had a magic for me. I was unaware then of its remarkable similarity to the other fortress town, Terezín, my future prison-home.

During the secret lectures and discussions in Terezín, on the history of art, literature, religion and philosophy, those stolen hours at home proved useful indeed, as I had spent them going through the family's huge library, book by book. I also had my own way of expanding my knowledge beyond the lessons in the *Mädchenheim*. I combined pleasure with learning by studying with my admirers. I chose my partner according to what I needed to know. Beneath the pear tree in the courtyard of the *Mädchenheim*, one of them taught me French pronunciation, while another recited Karel Čapek's translations of Verlaine or Rimbaud and I wrote down the poems in a little notebook. These courtiers of mine were six or eight years older than I. They were intelligent and patiently put up with my whims and my rejection of their sexual overtures. Sadly, not one of them resembled my childhood idol Gary Cooper.

One day, I realised that I really was jealous of the girls who went out with less intellectual boys who were more handsome than my companions. I decided that I would switch from brains to beauty. I would try to find such a handsome boy that the other girls would stare with envy and admiration.

My Adonis's name was Honza. I don't remember how we met. His job in the ghetto was a coveted one, as he was a cook. But that was not the reason why I returned his affection. I really did like him very much. After three days we already held hands and I was almost falling in love. But bad luck struck. A scarlet fever epidemic broke out and I caught it.

I was admitted to the main hospital and placed in an overcrowded room on the ground floor. Outside, below the barred window, I had plenty of visitors. One of my courtiers brought me the second volume of Goethe's *Faust* when I was able to climb out of bed and collect it. Inspired, I read for hours and hours. I don't know how far I understood its complicated philosophy. I was proud that I could actually read it and showed off about it for a long time afterwards.

Instead of *Faust*, my Honza brought me various Terezín titbits. In a small can there was a real delicacy: a sort of custard made of black, watery coffee with pieces of margarine and thickened with potato starch. This creamy liquid was often the main meal at noon on Fridays and it was poured on the top layer of the mess-tin over a little baked sweet dumpling. I was certain that after the war this would be my favourite delicacy. Honza put the tin through the bars, stroked my fingers and gazed at me, his almond-coloured eyes filled with love. We did not talk much, and then, tired out, I returned to bed.

155

After several weeks I left the hospital and, still feeling weak, I returned to the *Mädchenheim*. Honza and I then met in typical ghetto style, just like all the other young couples. There was only one place where it was possible to see some grass and green bushes, and which was also fairly deserted. That was the path behind the Cavalier Barracks, the prison for the mad.

It was spring and tiny leaves adorned a few of the bushes. Honza and I had to contend with the agonised shufflings and screams of the inmates, which made our hearts ache. When we glimpsed hands squeezing the window bars, *our* hands separated. We were almost ashamed that we were young and healthy.

Honza lived in the men's barracks, the Sudeten. I was able to go there, sit with him on his bunk and embrace him. Some of the men had made a hessian curtain from sacks to give the illusion of a little privacy for them and for their wives or girlfriends. But that was not enough for me. I was too young and self-conscious, so I could not ignore the hundreds of people around the three-tiered bunks in the large barracks.

In our free time after work, Honza and I mostly talked. He patiently listened as, in most minute detail, I described my room at home – explaining, for example, that from the window you could see the flowering cherry in May and hear the sounds of a piano or violin carry across the garden from the music school next to our house. Honza began to lose patience, though, when I enthusiastically started to relate the plot of *The Forsyte Saga* or *The Well of Loneliness*. Enough was enough.

'This doesn't interest me at all. If you want to see what I really enjoy, come to the barracks courtyard between six and seven today because we are going to play football.'

I accepted his preference – even my beloved grandfather occasionally visited the Mnichovo Hradiště football ground and ardently supported the game.

'The ground isn't the right size,' Honza explained to me, 'but somehow we have adjusted to this.'

In Terezín that was not surprising. Many things were 'somehow', just as they were in a normal world – from playing a piano with no legs, set on planks, to dying in humiliating conditions. The variations on the theme 'somehow' were unending but they helped us to live. In the Terezín fortress, as long as one did not die, life continued 'somehow' and football was played on an irregular football ground. It was just that the footballer here was a prisoner with an empty stomach and today, tomorrow, or the day after, his winning goal could be, and probably was, his last.

Not so long before, my footballer had scraped through college and then, like many other Jewish boys and girls, learned a trade. In the ghetto he managed to get into the kitchen where no qualifications were required. I wanted him to tell me that he did not steal food. He tried to explain to me that if he brought some extra morsels to his sick friends, that was more moral than if he did nothing. I did not know how to cope with this, and the moral values that had been instilled at home took a battering. Ultimately I was glad that, together with the other sick people in the scarlet fever ward, I had tasted the custard Honza brought.

I tried unsuccessfully to persuade Honza to improve his education. How could this boy have completed matriculation? In May, for my birthday, he gave me a wonderful present: shoes, which had been made secretly in workshops that supplied the SS; shoes with high wooden soles, and uppers of black leather cut out like sandals. Undoubtedly Honza had exchanged food for them. I never wore them in Terezín, because such shoes adorned the feet of girls who received them for favours which I was still not prepared to give. Those shoes must have cost a fortune – at least two loaves of bread or a cube of margarine. Honza gave the shoes to me with such pleasure that I accepted them. It was not until after the war that I began wearing them, as a tribute to Honza and as two small reminders of our friendship.

It was much later on, well after he had perished somewhere in Poland, that I realised just how fine he had been. At sixteen years of age I did not fully appreciate his enthusiasm – such enthusiasm that after ten-hour shifts in the kitchen he could find the strength to kick a corner. I did not value his light-heartedness, his playfulness and sense of humour. The fact is, it wasn't Honza who was my first love in the ghetto.

The capacity for love is always present, at all times and everywhere, but circumstances change the way in which this potential is realised. They say 'love always finds a way, love overcomes all obstacles' and, yes, even in the ghetto, finding love remained a potent possibility, strengthening people's hopes for the present and the future. When it was found it was often snuffed out before it could blaze, but in ghetto life even an hour of happiness seemed a long time. Time is always a relative concept and time and place were vitally important in my first experience of love. Is it possible to speak unemotionally about such a time? Can one speak without sentimentality?

One evening, early in July, I returned with my work group to the ghetto. We had been working in the intense summer heat in the fields between Terezín and Litoměřice, near the Small Fortress. It had been a hard, sweaty day. I was comforted by the pleasant prospect that, after a few more steps, the gates of the *Mädchenheim* would close behind me. I could sprawl on my bunk and not budge. A day in the hot fields, from 6 a.m. to 6 p.m., was long enough. In the morning, we had the usual coffee substitute; at noon, two to three potatoes, mostly half-rotten, with a spoonful of swedes; and in the evening, thin, powdered, greyish-green lentil soup. In the weeks of harvesting we supplemented our diet by stealing whatever we could. It was a risk, but who wouldn't try?

In that first week of July, I was not laden with stolen food. We had been tossing hay, which always smells delicious but is quite inedible. Dirty and hungry, I looked forward to a mess-tin of hot soup. The last thing on my mind was my appearance. My eyes ached from the bright sun and rested on the soothing green grass of the square. Five young men were cutting the half-grown grass with machine-like precision. My gaze became riveted upon one of them. How was it possible that in two years of working in the fields I had not met him? After only a glimpse I would have noticed him.

In fact, he had only recently arrived at the ghetto from Panenské Břežany. He cut the grass precisely and with great concentration. I ran my hand through my unruly, dark brown curly hair, trying to give it some shape. With the back of my hand, I wiped the sweat from my forehead and felt that I had smeared it with dust. He did not notice me, or how I stared at him. He was wearing only work trousers and, from the waist up, his body was brown from the sun. He had a narrow head and light brown, wavy hair. I couldn't see his eyes, but I knew that here was my ideal man.

He paused a few steps from me and must have felt that someone was observing him. He raised his head and golden flecks shone from his eyes. After a surfeit of romantic novels, I was contemptuous of 'love at first sight', but suddenly love at first sight seemed a reality. He gave me a big smile – and, of course, he had perfect teeth.

'Hello there, do we know each other?' he asked.

'No-o-o,' I stammered, 'but I do farm work, too, and I live over there in the *Mädchenheim.*'

'Do you want something?' he asked me pleasantly. He could see that I was rooted to the spot.

'No-o-o, nothing, I'm terribly grubby and I must go and have a shower. We have a shower, you know. It's wonderful, even if it's cold.'

To myself I was saying, 'This one is not for me, he must have plenty of girls, better keep away. But, then, what the heck?' Something inside me rebelled. 'There are plenty of men who are interested in me. They're musicians and actors. Surely I'm not going to tremble in front of some good-looking farmhand?'

The man with shining eyes went on cutting the grass. I wanted to run away, but my legs felt like lead while my mind was spinning. Now I will have to pay dearly for my virginity. Everyone's scared of a virgin. Apparently the boys say keep away from them, they are much more of a problem than a pleasure. Besides, true love doesn't belong here where love is short-lived and even the longest affairs last only two or three months, until the next transports. Each inhabitant has already had more than enough tragedy and misfortune. Love during the war? In the ghetto? Pure bad luck.

He finished cutting his stretch of grass, turned around and walked towards me. I was panic-stricken. 'I'll run away,' I thought. But I didn't.

As soon as he reached me I blurted out the last thing I would have expected of myself: 'Are you free some time?'

To my fascinated horror I heard, 'Of course. Come over tomorrow to the cellar on Q 7. I live in a sort of dump there with a friend. My name is Milan.'

Next day, I woke up with a glowing feeling of happiness. The sun had relocated itself in my heart, in my whole mind and body. 'I'll see Milan today!'

I jumped up, pulled on my overalls and I only remember that my group had to march out with rakes on our shoulders. We dried hay again that day but I was not aware of anything around me, not even the girls teasing me. Several times I almost stumbled over the rake.

'Our fastidious and prim girl has fallen in love on us!' The girls enjoyed themselves at my expense all day. The small pile of hay, which

I had always been able to toss onto the horse-drawn cart, fell back on my head. The girls guffawed.

I ignored them. I looked blissfully and disbelievingly into the distance across the Ohře river. Pink clouds floated in the sky, much pinker, I was sure, than usual.

After work, we marched back from the fields around Terezín, almost jogging, in fact, just as the Nazis had instructed. To and from the gate we were escorted by the local police and they had to trot with us. On that day, however, it seemed to me that we were dragging along.

Free time was still allocated: about two hours in the winter, between 6 and 8 in the evening, while in summer it was between 6 and 9. In that time, I had to gulp down my portion of soup, have a shower, and find something to wear. I raced to my room on the first floor of L 410.

'Girls, I need something good to wear.'

As I mentioned earlier, our commune shared clothing. Whoever had an invitation took priority. But of course I now had to listen to mocking comments. I used to have fits of morality and now the girls were enjoying paying me back. But I was racing against time, so I didn't even answer their taunts.

Finally I stood in front of his house in Q Street, the street where my family and I had begun our Terezín life. Now everything was different. I sneaked into the worn-out, gloomy house and went down the even dingier steps to the cellar. In wooden cubicles, where the original inhabitants had stored coal, were tiny rooms. Wooden doors made of battens were covered over on the inside with hessian sacks. On the outside of the doors were some cards and one of them said 'Milan and Franta'. It was so quiet that my own breathing scared me. I knocked. The door opened and a tall, very thin woman, much older than my seventeen years, poked her head out. I heard her say, 'Milan asked me to wait here for you, he didn't know when he would get back from work.'

My head was spinning, but I went in and sat down on the edge of a sort of couch. A woman. And it's as if she's at home here. They are not badly off. Everyone longs for this kind of privacy in Terezín. How did he come by this?

It really was more like a coalshed than a room. In it were two bunks like couches. Above them were two sketches, which I still have. Behind one couch was a shelf made from roughly hewn planks and on it was a small wooden candlestick, a candle and a book.

Panicking, I stood up to leave – but suddenly he was there. He beamed, he was radiant. He looked like a hero from an American film. With perfect manners, he introduced me to 'his girl Marie' and my feeling of being in a film intensified. Marie was a pretty, self-confident woman.

From its hiding place, Milan pulled out an electric cooker, something which was forbidden and punishable by death. He invited me to have some tea. I sat on the edge of the couch, held a china cup full of tea and felt as if this was a dream. Yet it was all quite different from my daydreaming, which seemed to have been unimaginative.

In a hoarse voice I stuttered, 'I have to leave ...' But Marie moved before I could. She withdrew politely and disappeared. I was mesmerised, as if by a spell, and sank down again.

Milan, this handsome, mature man, took me by the hand.

'Marie is a wonderful woman,' he said. 'She is completely alone in the ghetto. Her husband was deported about a year ago and she hasn't received any news about him. She's a teacher and a woman who can cope with anything, but, unfortunately, she's jealous. So, I wanted her to see you. She could then see that such a young girl isn't for me and isn't a threat to her.'

He could hardly have said anything worse. Didn't he see that I was an adult and that I too was a woman who could cope with anything? And then I heard myself say this nonsense out loud. Transports, cattle wagons, hard labour, hunger, nothing existed except my awakening love and a woman's jealousy.

Milan began laughing. But so nicely that I was not angry. I knew myself that I was being ridiculous. He gave me a kiss on the forehead and gently pushed me through the door into the darkness of the main cellar. I staggered out to the street. Whatever would I do about my feelings?

Having decided to take Milan from Marie, I hurried over to Q 7 every spare moment. The little room was never locked. Sometimes I bumped into Milan's roommate, Franta, and then I left quickly. At other times no one was home and so I stayed. I lay down on Milan's bed, read his books, hugged his pillow. When he appeared and we were alone, I droned on repetitively, like an organ-grinder's tune.

'Marie is too old for you and she's not even pretty.'

This was untrue. Normally I was shy, but now I became pushy, provocative and possessive. I hardly recognised myself. I didn't realise that my behaviour could scare him off. Several times, Milan politely threw me out. But after a few days I was in the cellar again. I volunteered for the hardest work in the fields only when I thought he might be there. Dignity, on which I had previously prided myself, had disappeared.

In terms of a Terezín time span, the course of conquest was taking a considerable time. Fourteen days? Three weeks? A month? I do not know. Then it happened. A wild summer storm raged, the sky opened and water cascaded down. We were even escorted from the fields earlier than usual. Just as I was, soaked to the skin, I raced through the empty streets to Q 7.

He was alone. He embraced me gently.

'Marie and I have parted,' he said. 'I love you.'

He kissed me.

Much later on I was told that Marie had tried to commit suicide. Why not? I could understand that. But I had neither the willpower nor the time to be compassionate.

The autumn of that year, 1944, which saw the virtual depopulation of Terezín, came far too early. We had only three months of love – a love that was gentle, joyous and deadly serious. From childhood, Milan's family had called him 'sunshine' and, later, his friends did as well. He radiated warmth as he walked unscathed through a sad, evil world, and he always knew how to delight the people around him. On many occasions I convinced myself that not only I, because of my love, perceived him in this way, but others did as well, even men.

At seventeen I was more than grown up. From the age of twelve I had lived through situations that had accelerated my maturity. Now, with Milan, came the powerful longing to discover my body, to become fully a woman.

He explained patiently why he did not want this to occur.

'You are just seventeen,' ran his chief argument. 'Neither of us knows whether you or I will leave on a transport. But we do know that if you become pregnant, it means death. And even if you don't, you will be emotionally attached to someone whom you may never see again.'

I tried to seduce him. Inside me, longings had been aroused about which I formerly had no inkling. I tempted him so much that he moaned with desire but, at the last moment, he always resisted.

'No and no! If I were seventeen ... but I'm an adult, and because I love you I must behave responsibly.'

He hushed my pleadings and desperate cries by gently placing his hand on my mouth. He held me to him and in that embrace there was everything from tenderness to passion. Futile longing only heightened my emotions so that in those moments I felt that we almost reached the edge of infinity. This unfulfilled desire tied me to him for many years, and perhaps affected my whole life – certainly my marriage.

The news that the Germans were losing on all fronts had reached the ghetto. Hope grew. Perhaps we would survive? These raised hopes made it worse when we learned of the autumn transports. On 23 September, 2,500 men up to the age of fifty were summoned. The summons, stipulating a certain age group for a work transport, seemed genuine. It was only after the war that this, like other deceptions, was discovered. The narrow pieces of paper with one's official number, the day and time when to board the train, were always ominous. This time the explanation was 'your wives and children will follow you, once you have prepared a place for them. Take only a small bag and food for one day. All your needs are at your destination: Dresden.'

That promise of future contact with people left in Terezín consolidated the illusion. The SS command took over the whole organisation of this transport from the Jewish Council, so that the possibility of evasion was eliminated.

The time for departure came and, with it, the long, long trains with their freight cars. In each wagon there were 70–90 people and the trains left two or three times weekly. Gradually even those in privileged positions disappeared never to return, because they knew far too much. We all desperately hoped that the autumn chain of transports would be the last.

It was not. Another night would come, and with it, the narrow strips of tissue-paper with the numbers and the times of boarding. Nightmares were not dreamt, they were lived. Who? When? Where to?

The transports dominated everything; nothing else was important. The dreadful waiting. Bunks emptied. Until now, life in the ghetto, with a little imagination, could have been called 'normal', but that had ended. Doctors, nurses and patients had left the central and auxiliary hospitals. The aged and ill who remained were left to their own fate.

This continued throughout October. On 28 October, the remaining members of the Jewish Council, the *Ältestenrat*, departed on the transport. Those Jews who, under instructions from the SS, had thrown the ashes of almost 30,000 people into the Ohře river, vanished. Time and again the transports reduced the number of Terezín prisoners. At the beginning of September 1944 there had been relatively few people left (29,500, mostly from Bohemia and Moravia), but by the end of October there were just 11,000 of us.

Our *Mädchenheim* was not, of course, exempt from the transports. The rooms became more and more deserted as friends and acquaintances packed their small bags. Our carers, as well as the girls, received their summonses.

I myself received that little slip of paper several times. It meant walking to the gates of the Hamburg Barracks at three in the morning. By chance, I was always withdrawn. Once, I had a high temperature and in that particular transport the ill were rejected. On another occasion, agricultural workers were needed for the autumn harvest. I was among them. On yet another occasion, other girls and I had to stay and peel off strips of mica under the direct supervision and 'protection' of the SS, so that it could be reprocessed for the German air industry. Another time, my mother saved us both.

I didn't feel joy about these escapes, only sadness. My closest friends and others went and I remained. Why? Staying did not bring happiness. It brought only sorrow and a guilty conscience.

After Alenka's departure, I moved into a different room, going from the ground floor to the first floor of the house on L 410. There was a likable bunch of girls there, but I was a 'foreigner', a newcomer, an intruder. I have the feeling that each room had its established core which was held very firmly together and those who were relocated after a transport were outsiders. Girls from different rooms did not mix much. In my new room I found myself on the third level of bunks which again occupied the whole area of the room, apart from a square in the middle. Here I found Miriam who, after Alenka, became my closest friend.

Miriam was quite plump. Her chubby, baby-pink and white cheeks were framed by thick, curly, black hair, and she had large dark eyes and a button nose. She said what she thought, she was kind and, seemingly, uncomplicated. But that was only a façade. A good-natured exterior concealed an exceptionally intelligent mind and a very sensitive, restless nature. Miriam's plumpness singled her out from the other girls, whose proportions more accurately represented the paltry food allowance. She was not the only unnaturally large girl in the ghetto. There were plenty of other women and girls like that. It was said that either it was a hormonal irregularity after menstruation ceased, or perhaps the Nazis put arsenic in our food (in the same way as it is given to horses when they are taken to market). I don't know. What I do know is that Miriam suffered because of her appearance. Perhaps that was what brought us together? I wasn't as thin as a wraith either. Miriam did not like her bloated body and I understood this perfectly.

She was sixteen, came from Wallachia (Moravia) and was a committed Zionist. She had no doubts that Jews should live in Palestine and that, straight after the war, she would move there. In her pocket she had some pieces of paper with Hebrew words on them; that is, modern Hebrew words. She wanted to teach me but came up against my innate Czechness. She belonged to the Left and was among those who believed that the Soviet Union would spread socialism to save humanity. She was even learning Russian, and that was somewhat closer to my interests. So she taught me the Cyrillic alphabet, some Russian poems, and how to speak the language a little. Incidentally, there were many girls and teachers in the home who looked to the east, to Russia, with hope. A sad irony.

Miriam sometimes sat cross-legged on the floor, or high up on the bunks, with me next to her, at lectures or seminars in the *Mädchenheim*. She devoured everything, asked questions and wrote avidly. She craved knowledge from those who brought to Terezín not only sacks and eiderdowns but heads full of painting, music, literature, philosophy and mathematics.

It was with Miriam that I shared the little box for catching fleas and successfully entered the competition to catch the most. I don't know how long our close friendship lasted, whether it was for weeks or months after Alenka's departure. Again, time is relative. I know that I was very fond of her, but she liked me even more. She wanted my exclusive attention and affection, and was jealous of everything and everyone. I tried to be understanding because I had both my parents in Terezín and she had nobody. I also had boys who wrote poems to me and whom I could go out with; Miriam did not. She only had me. When I genuinely, deeply and passionately fell in love, it was terrible for her. That last Terezín summer was ardent and wonderful for me. It was hopelessly sad for Miriam. She was desperately angry with me. The person closest to her lived for something and somebody else.

In September and October 1944 the number of transports going east rose to the highest number in Terezín's history. Incredibly, my father, my lover, and my friend received their summonses simultaneously.

For the two days before the transport's departure I ran, in a state of wretchedness, from courtyard to courtyard of the Hamburg Barracks, where the selected prisoners had been taken. Two of the three doomed people could do nothing to ease my misery. Father was distressed that at any moment I would leave him. And Miriam? She said: 'Either you are my friend and love me and will spend these last hours here with me, and only with me, or I don't want to see or know you ever again.'

She was deadly serious and I certainly believed her. Her words sounded like a curse.

'If she returns, she will never forgive me,' I said to myself. I begged her to understand what I was enduring. I felt terribly sad that as her friend, and at such a time, I could not say that I loved her exclusively.

These were days full of anguish. I had the feeling that, on this occasion, perhaps the most important of my life, I was doing everything badly. I had deeply hurt Miriam. Father had quietly withdrawn into himself, although his attention was actually focused on Mother, his adored wife. In a moment, Milan was about to disappear from my life. A solitary sentence rang through my head: 'How and why do I go on living?'

Mother and I had managed to sneak into the Hamburg Barracks. My heart had thumped with anxiety. Father sat on a case in one of the barracks courtyards, while Milan had been assigned to a room into which hundreds of people had been squeezed. Miriam was on the first floor with a crowd of completely unknown women. Where to first? What could I do that was fair?

I went to Milan first. Towards morning, I went to my father and he said, 'What sort of a daughter are you? How can you leave me even for a moment?' It was terrible.

And then Miriam, who spoke very softly, so that no one else would hear. 'I will never forgive you that you are not staying with me!'

It was dreadful. I told neither Father nor Miriam that I was going back to Milan. I knew that it would hurt them both even more.

Milan sat on a straw mattress in a corner with his friends. In those few moments together, we embraced, our fingers entwined and we looked at each other. We did not speak. He pulled a small leather case out of his pocket and pressed it into my hand. I opened it. In the middle was a small photo of him at home. Someone had snapped him with one leg stretched forward as he ran a race. On the white edge around the photograph he had written, 'I am leaving. I love you. I will return.' The increasing tension of those days and nights reached a climax and I sobbed loudly. He held me and soothed me like a small child. He said, 'You will see that in this race I will be among those who finish.'

Eventually I stopped sobbing and was able to go back to my father. The courtyard was empty. I turned around and raced back. I must see Milan again. But at the entrance to the room where, a few moments ago, he had embraced me, stood the SS guards and their dogs. Men with yellow stars on their chests began to march across the courtyard, to the gates leading to the ramps from where the trains left. As ever, in the hours before the wagons were sealed, it was dangerous to be nearby. If it seemed to the SS that the wagons were not full enough, extra people were hunted down and shoved into them.

As that horrible dawn approached, the SS guards' boots thundered through the empty courtyards. At the last moment, I helped Mother climb into a huge rubbish bin in the corner of the yard to wait until the transport departed. With several other people, I ran until we reached the doors to the large cellar below the barracks. The doors shut behind us and we groped around in the dark towards a sliver of light in the distance. It was the little cellar window. As this wasn't the first time I had been there I knew that if we were able to find a plank of some kind, or a chair, or anything that would enable us to step up, we would see through the window right onto the ramp. That is how I had seen Irenka Krausová and Karel Švenk vanish into the cattle wagons.

It was always horrifying. But this morning was the worst. Somewhere over there my friend, my father, and my first love had all disappeared.

At last I too held a summons in my hand. This time no one would recall me! I had even said it out loud to the few girls remaining in our room. They thought I had gone crazy. But no, I was quite sane; not only sane, I was glad. At last I would not miss out. I would follow the others. We truly did not know what was happening so far away.

I ran to find Mother, to tell her my news. She also held a narrow slip of paper. Again, we received the deceptive assurance that the next transport, which consisted of women and children, would be welcomed by the men who would be waiting for us.

Mother was glad that we were going together. On my right wrist I had a large ulcer. Pus and blood seeped from it and stained the rather flimsy bandage. My arm was very painful and Mother seemed genuinely sorry for me. We still had a few hours left before assembling. Mother accompanied me to the *Mädchenheim* to help me pack my rucksack, because I could not move my arm. She put it in a sling and was really kind; I felt quite moved. Previously, everyone had looked after *her* – Father or I, or someone else. Mother was always the one who was cared for. And now she was looking after me. It was quite unexpected. My tears of affection were mixed with tears of joy. Finally, I was going.

Mother and I walked through the gate of the Hamburg Barracks, rucksacks on our backs. We did not have to creep around furtively: this time we belonged there. Then for hours and hours we stood in orderly lines in one of the courtyards. There were about a thousand women and children, the average number of people in a transport. The Nazis loved order and kept our rows ruler-straight. The command was that heads were to be lowered. We could only see SS Obersturmführer Rahm's shiny boots as he paced the courtyard with long strides. I stood somewhere in the middle of the first long row; my mother was exactly behind me in the second row. Shortly, dawn would break. We stood and stood. In each corner of the yard, high above us, shone piercing floodlights.

My right arm hung limply in its sling and was almost unbearably painful. I still have a scar from that ulcer. Mother continually whispered something to me from behind because she was frantic that I would not survive several days' travelling with an infected arm. I, however, was only interested in the fact that we were following the others, following my Milan. My thoughts wandered far away ... it was a matter of days since Milan embraced me so agonisingly but wonderfully.

A thump from behind roused me from my dream. It was my mother. She had violently poked me just as Rahm walked past. I jerked out from the line. The SS commander glared incredulously. He thrust his chin forward to shout. But my still-beautiful mother was already standing next to me and in perfect German said very loudly, 'My daughter cannot leave, she wouldn't survive the journey; she has an infected arm. I cannot go either because I must look after her.'

I do not think that this camp commandant, this arbiter of life and death, had ever heard such an absurd statement. I could feel how the throng of people behind me were shrinking in horror. What would happen? What would they inflict on us all for this impertinence?

This cruel and treacherous man, black-uniformed from head to toe, teetered. Silently, he looked at us, one and then the other. After a seemingly interminable silence, he stated in a harsh voice, '*Die Mutter und die Tochter bleiben hier!*' (mother and daughter stay here).

Karl Rahm's thumb pointed to the corner of the yard. My burning body refused to budge. Mother took me by the shoulders and led me to the spot he had indicated. We stood there for an inordinate length of time. The transport of women and children, most of whom were going from these ramps to the gas chambers, left. *Die Mutter und die Tochter* stayed.

The transports from Terezín ceased. In the days and weeks, even months, following, every fragment of joy dwindled. I was filled with sullen sadness all the time. I was not in the least grateful to my mother for her quick-witted action. I avoided her and was almost nasty to her. My anger towards her didn't wane but became quite unreasonable. Mother's meddling had left me without Milan, without Father, without friends. What I *was* left with was a guilty conscience because of the abandoned bunks. Why them and not me?

It was mostly women who remained in the ghetto. The Jewish Council's artificially built structure had collapsed. Cooks, men, doctors and nurses, wardens and our own wonderful carers – all had gone. There were only sick people and even more hunger. By the winter of 1944–45, the ghetto had finally become a desolate place, just as the Germans had planned. The hearses that had been brought to Terezín from far and wide to provide the main form of transport – for bread as well as corpses – fulfilled their purpose to an even greater degree.

What were we waiting for? Why go on?

During this last winter of the war everyone – adults, adolescents, even children – had to do whatever was necessary. I worked alongside girls I did not know. We loaded, lugged and unloaded enormous tree trunks. For days on end, I shovelled wagons of coke to be used for heating the Nazis' quarters and their hotel-casino. I cut up willow sticks on the damp and windy meadows around the Ohře river. For a few weeks, I had to weave straw mats for covering the glasshouses in the Nazis' gardens.

Would we still be here in spring? Would the war never end? The harder the work, the more grateful I was. It saved me. Days filled with sadness and apprehension hurried by faster. I do not know how other people endured that winter. I survived by an act of my imagination, longing to vanish. I wove mats and, in the large frame, wove my dreams into the straw. I imagined meadows of dandelions in which Milan and I had not made love, unknown countryside where we had never been. I heard the powerful Verdi *Requiem* in my head, the requiem performance during which we had not held hands. I recited Rimbaud's poetry to myself, poetry we had had no time to read together. The burden of unfulfilled love was huge.

In that winter, the chapters of my childhood and adolescence definitely concluded. The last remnants of a childlike faith in goodness, justice and truth vanished. This was the legacy of the last winter of the war. There was nobody to play the old harmonium in the brewery attic, or the ruined piano that rested on planks. There was no one to act in the Klicper or Langer plays, no one to sing Karel Švenk's Terezín Anthem. It all seemed so long ago since we heard the last bars of *The Bartered Bride* fade away.

Now the *Mädchenheim* was abandoned and its gate was boarded up. I moved to a room in a house with Mother and six unknown women. There was plenty of room everywhere now. Space, which we used to long for, was now far too great.

A taste of freedom

Questions were hanging in the air. Who and what awaited us after the war? We had fearful suspicions of what lay ahead, but we did not know that the coming reality would be even worse.

We felt vindictive as we watched the trains departing from the ramps behind the Hamburg Barracks. This time, however, they carried freight, not human beings. The SS were packing up. The prisoners, with revolvers pointed at their backs, nailed down huge crates full of stolen goods. The direction the Nazis headed for was west, away from the Russians. They still had weapons, soldiers and dogs, and we were still surrounded by ramparts, barbed wire and locked gates. They had the power to do anything with us. In spite of that, our fear of them had lessened.

One day, perhaps at the end of April or beginning of May, 1945, someone created a stir. 'The Russians are here, the liberators are coming,' was the word spread around Terezín. From the barracks windows we joyously waved at the Soviet soldiers in their fur caps. Their horses and carts were small, and the soldiers themselves looked exhausted. They shouted, 'Greetings!' We rejoiced. Those who could, ran out onto the square towards the German headquarters.

'The war is over, it's over,' was heard from all directions. Suddenly, it was not just individuals, but a united crowd. The throng, driven by some invisible strength, moved slowly towards the wooden fence that still separated us from the Germans. Suddenly, one tall SS guard appeared by himself in front of us. He waved his pistol and shouted something. The crowd's reaction was weird. It quietened but, step by step, the first rows moved closer to him. No one wavered, even though the pistol was aimed as high as our heads. Then a miracle happened. It was the guard who turned on his heels and ran! The end of the war was really here.

Later, we learnt that the Russian army which gave us such courage actually consisted of troops who were allies of the German, not the Soviet, empire. Karl Rahm, the SS commander in Terezín since early 1944, had been captured. Before his execution in Litoměřice, he defended himself with the claim that, thanks to him, the building of gas chambers in Terezín (February 1945) had been delayed.

Trains returned from the east to Terezín and brought people who walked in the death marches. The state of the people we helped from the cattle wagons defies description. We tried to prop up those human wrecks against the walls, so that we could give them spoonfuls of tea. They did not even have the strength to sit up. They had come from various concentration camps in Poland and Germany.

In the first weeks of May, doctors and nurses came voluntarily from Prague to help cope with the situation in Terezín. The doctors instructed us that for at least three days we must not give those near death anything other than sweetened tea. Any solid food could kill them, even a slice of bread. It was very hard, for they pleaded with their eyes, hands and mouths. Yet those who succumbed to their pleas were killers. A person who had survived for weeks on mud and grass must not eat. We experienced days of horror as, among that mass of ashen skin and bone, we tried to recognise our own relatives and friends.

The look of burnt-out eyes, apathy and immobility disappeared extraordinarily quickly. In two or three days these people were returning to life. Would I recognise my father, my aunts and uncles, cousins? Would I recognise Milan? Who would come back to me?

On the third day of this sad yet uplifting task of searching, as I tried to conceal the horror I felt, one of these skeletons glanced at me and his eyes gleamed. In the state he was in I could not even guess his age. I did not know him. Or did I? His first words took my breath away.

'I am Zdeněk. You don't know me, but I know you. While I was in Terezín, I watched you from a distance because I admired you so much. I cannot really believe that it is you who is reviving me. I am so happy – you'll see, after a few days I will be all right. And once I have had a shave ...'

His eyes were sunken, his face emaciated, he had a stubble beard and a prickly growth of light brown hair on his shaved head. I honestly could not remember him and, even if I could, I would not have recognised him. I hugged him, kissed his rough cheeks and clasped his bony hand. I couldn't avoid the thought of how happy I would be if it were Milan whom I could embrace. Fortunately Zdeněk was so full of joy that we had met, he did not notice my tremor of disappointment.

Zdeněk was indeed up and about in no time. He did not utter one sentence of what he had lived through. He looked to the future, a future which included me. Whenever I had time I went to the improvised hospital where he was resting. Later on, we walked on the ramparts from which, not so long ago, we were banned. The lilac trees and cherry blossoms were blooming. It was spring and the grass was turning green. Did life only wake up in nature? Or would it awaken in me, and in us all? On those walks, Zdeněk gently held my hand and kissed me. I did not know how to refuse him.

Among those who returned to Terezín, I did not find my father, or Milan, or any of my relatives and friends.

Terezín, during those days of May, with its first taste of freedom (however half-hearted and bleak for us), was still a dangerous place. A new typhoid epidemic raged. Officially, the ghetto was defunct, but not much had changed. We were stuck in quarantine, and Czech police now guarded us. They were friendly, but we were still prisoners.

Hundreds of people died of typhus on the threshold of their freedom. I volunteered to assist in the buildings which housed the sick. Perhaps I wanted to do something that was vitally important. Above all, however, I wanted to escape from myself and become immersed in activities that would distract me from the agony of waiting. I hardly saw my mother at that time. I do not even know where she was or what she was doing. I had the feeling that I was alone on this post-war path back to life and that I was returning to freedom with empty hands and an empty heart.

On 9 May 1945 the war ended in Czechoslovakia. The Germans surrendered. In defiance of the typhoid quarantine, the Czech police allowed many people to escape in the following days. Along with Mariane, a girl I met during the epidemic, I decided to escape. It was not difficult. A few words, a smile and a plea were sufficient for a policeman to look the other way.

After the years of imprisonment behind the ramparts in the ghetto, we stood on the road and it was up to us alone to decide which direction to take. Well then, to Prague. The first truck we waved at stopped. It was obvious where we had come from and instead of offering his hand, the driver gave us a piece of buttered bread. He apologised that there was no room in the cabin, but we could sit comfortably in the back among the boxes. The countryside, with no wire barriers, trees along the country road, a strong wind blowing, and *buttered bread*, at last enabled us to feel the great happiness and joy of freedom.

Mariane and I suddenly found ourselves in revolutionary Prague, full of people and chaos. Neither she nor I knew Prague well. But we each had a vague idea where to go. We wished each other luck, hugged, and went our separate ways. We never met again.

I asked the way to the suburb of Smíchov. I had no money, but in any case the trams weren't running. It took me quite a long time to reach the house in Smíchov where my mother's brother, my wonderful Uncle Vilík, had had his bachelor apartment. Vilík was well-educated, a sportsman, a humanist and a freemason. He had been the manager of a small bank, but I don't think that it was the main thing in his life. He was a social democrat, and as soon as the German occupation began he had become involved in underground work. I know nothing more than that he unselfishly helped many people and that his friends called him The Scarlet Pimpernel.

When my parents and I had first been in Terezín it was Vilík who had sent us short, daily reassurances on the official letter cards. It was he who organised the network of people who sent us those half-kilogram parcels of food, soap, toothpaste and things. As I explained earlier, the network included my friend Violet until the Gestapo seized her, though I do not know how she and my uncle had become acquainted. When we stopped receiving the little parcels and letters from my grandparents and then, later, from Vilík, we suspected that something terrible had happened. Our suspicions were correct. The Gestapo had taken Vilík from his apartment in Smíchov some time in 1943.

Now I stood in front of the house where my uncle had lived, my heart filled with anxiety. I knew the caretaker, Mrs Žejdlíková, well. For years she had looked after Vilík, as if he were her own son. I rang the bell. The miracle happened: it was Mrs Žejdlíková who opened the door. Her kind face froze and then she began crying.

'So you are alive? I heard ... the opposite. For a long time I have had no news of Mr Bondy. What I do know is not good. I have been

trying to find out if he returned from the prison in Buchenwald. Apparently a bus load of people has come from there.'
I was unable to speak. Kind Mrs Žejdlíková put her arms around me. 'After your uncle's arrest, a German officer took his apartment and everything in it. A few weeks ago he disappeared, but most things were left in their right places. I have cleaned up in case Mr Bondy should return. You know what? I will open the apartment for you – the bed is newly made up and I will fill the bath. Have a wash, a good sleep and then let's see. I will bring you some tea, Renuška, and something to nibble.'

For more than two-and-a-half years I had not been in a bathroom, let alone in a bath of hot water, with sweet-smelling soap and a face cloth and a bath towel. I indulged myself completely, steeping in hot water. I closed my eyes and felt soothed. Mrs Žejdlíková dried me as if I were a small child and put me in a bed made up with fresh white linen. I immediately fell into a deep, dreamless sleep.

*

Return home? Where was my home? Who remained out of those we loved? How could anyone not think that it was incredible luck to survive, when so many others perished?

Unfortunately, it was not so simple. The lives of those people who, despite incredible odds, outlived millions, were full of bitterness. The struggle to reclaim a normal life again was immense.

In June 1945 I had nothing except a dark blue skirt, a white blouse, casual shoes, and some money which I received from Vilík's friends. I needed nothing else. From the safety of kind Mrs Žejdlíková's arms, I walked to the centre of Prague, to the Repatriation Office. I went there regularly for several days and read the lists of people accounted for by the Red Cross or the American and British armies: lists of those who had survived, those who had perished and those who were missing. Of course, it referred to only a fraction of the millions. Those of us who hung about in the hallway, hoping for miracles, continued to go there even when hope had gradually died away.

One day, I got tired of waiting. My uncle had not returned and there was no news of him, nor would there be, for many weeks, though he had in fact survived Buchenwald and would eventually reappear amongst us. I decided to go home, to Josefov, from where my family and I had been deported. I already knew that Grandmother had probably been exterminated and Grandfather had been shot. I did not want to even think about their house in Mnichovo Hradiště, the house where I had spent such happy years in my childhood.

Soviet officers were living in our apartment in Josefov. The apartment had been wrecked anyway, and I could not stay there. The revolutionary Czechoslovak National Council allocated to me a small flat which had previously been used by the Germans. It was awful, so strange and unfriendly. But I needed a base and an address where I could be found by those who looked for me and where Mother could stay when she returned.

It was from that address that I wrote my first letters as a free person. The first was to Violet (Jarmilka Holatová) and the second to Mother who was still in quarantine in Terezín. I felt guilty because I had fled from Terezín and had only left her a note. I didn't want to incur her disapproval.

'Dear Mama,

'I am very sorry if I have worried you. Please believe me, I could not have done anything else. Mama, don't ever think that you are not important to me.

'You know how impatient and unpleasant I was, mainly to you. I said to myself it's best if I do what I want. You must forgive me for having abandoned you surely it won't be for long. I managed to get to Prague in a truck with a friend. We were given some food. I walked to Smíchov. Vilík was imprisoned by the Gestapo, first in the Peček Palace, then in Buchenwald. So far, no one knows anything about him. Kind Mrs Žejdlíková welcomed me with open arms, gave me the keys to Vilík's flat and let me take a bath in his tub. A German officer had lived there until recently. He apparently stole some antiques and pictures, then disappeared. Mrs Žejdlíková had heard that none of us survived, so she was amazed when she saw me.

'In Prague, the girl with whom I had travelled, and I, elbowed our way through the crowds that had gone to Hradčany to welcome President Beneš. Prague is not damaged as much as I had expected. I am frightened of the masses of people and am constantly checking if I am wearing the star! Imagine that, now that I actually don't have to wear it! I still have it, but now it's of my own free will and that's completely different. I regularly go to the Repatriation Office to check if there is any news of Father or Vilík. I keep hoping about Grandma and Grandpa, Aunt Olga and simply everybody. Occasionally I meet someone from Terezín there. It is so strange, but they are the only people with whom I feel safe.

'Now can you believe this? Quite accidentally, I met one of our carers, Zdenka, who had been in Auschwitz and had exchanged a few words with Grandmother. It is not quite one year ago ... perhaps Grandma is still alive! Apparently when Grandfather and Grandmother were arrested they were treated very badly. I don't want to write about this as it may not even be true. Their apartment was plundered, first by the Germans and then by the Czechs including Mr Harvan from the house itself. Vilík was still free and so he had time to tell his friends. Grandma and Grandpa were arrested because they sent parcels to us in Terezín. Jarmilka Holatová was imprisoned as well and it seems that she hanged herself. I am so distressed by it all that I cannot share the joy of the crowds in the streets. I know nothing of Milan. There is no one at the address he gave me, the flat there is quite empty.

'Mama, you may not be pleased that I am telling you these things. But perhaps it's better that you prepare yourself a little for what awaits you here. I don't want to go back to Terezín. I am more use here. Vilík's acquaintances have offered me clothes, money and some help, as Vilík left a little money.

'Actually, I am writing to you from Josefov. I arrived last night and because there are Russian soldiers in our apartment, the National Council has temporarily given me a flat. It's terribly ugly, but I must have some sort of an address. I promise that as soon as the quarantine period ends in Terezín I'll arrange transport for you. I hope you'll congratulate me for having done so much, but perhaps not?

'Vilík's friends in Prague have found a job for me. Can you believe it? I can begin working straight away, as a nanny for 600 crowns a month, plus food, and with my own bathroom. What more could I wish for?

'The news about some of Vilík's friends is not particularly good. For example, the Blažeks, whom he liked so much, behaved very coldly after his arrest. Apparently they have many valuables of his, also some things from Mnichovo Hradiště. But not all people are the same. Mr Šulc was very sweet and gave me a box containing some rings.

'Mama dear, are you satisfied with me? Surely it is better that I am here and not idly waiting in that terrible Terezín? Please write to me immediately, and tell me that you are not cross with me. I will write every day.

'Kisses,
'Your Renka.'

I had been fifteen years old when I went to Terezín, and in the month of liberation I had completed my seventeenth year – in a similar fortress, Josefov. It was a strange feeling. The chestnut tree in the middle of the square was still there; the Theresan church, too, where I used to pray. The flat I was allotted, however, was at the opposite end of Josefov from my old home.

When the Russians found out from whom they had taken the apartment, they sent a soldier after me with a huge sack of clothing. In the sack there were pairs of shoes and even single ones. It reminded me of the other bundles which I had sorted under Mr Hermann's supervision at the beginning of my ghetto existence. I didn't unpack the bundle, but pushed it beneath the double bed. Another soldier came bringing bundles from the United Nations Relief and Rehabilitation Administration. These were full of chocolates, cigarettes, and tinned walnut spread. I was also invited to eat in the UNRRA canteen in Jaroměř. I was quite moved by this.

I went to the post office to send my letters to Mother and Violet. Some women were standing on the corner. In a rather bewildered way, one of them addressed me.

'Aren't you Renuška Friesová?'

I nodded, and then she uttered a sentence which I will never forget.

'So you returned? I heard that no one survived, so how did you?'

Perhaps I made a mistake when I inferred from her question that she actually meant what did we have to do to survive? Collaborate with the Germans? I knew that people imagined that the Nazis had seduced pretty girls, who had complied in order to live ...

I stood there speechless, feeling that I was standing in front of a jury of Josefov women. I said nothing. Surely I did not have to explain to her that if a German became sexually involved with a Jewish girl it would defile German racial purity and he would be punished? It probably happened, but not to anyone I knew.

Finally I said, 'I know nothing about my father and my other relatives. Mother and I survived, probably by chance. I don't know.'

With a quiet goodbye I walked away.

After that unpleasant encounter, I decided I would return to Prague, to kind Mrs Žejdlíková, and that I would continue going to the Repatriation Office. But two things happened. Quite unexpectedly my mother appeared at my new abode. Secondly, I received a letter.

As soon as Mother had received my news she had persuaded a policeman to release her from the still-quarantined ghetto. She wanted to look around and see what was left of our business and how to get it started again. I was very glad that I didn't have to sleep alone in that strange double bed.

The day after Mother's arrival, the letter came. The neat, school-girl handwriting on the envelope was familiar. Violet's? No, it was slightly different. Another Holat, Violet's sister, welcomed me back and begged me to come to them immediately if I wished to find Jarmilka (Violet) alive. The Germans had apparently released her from the prison at Jičín a few weeks previously, so that she could die at home.

I gave the letter to Mother and said I would leave straight away. Mother, who only just had the hazardous journey from Terezín behind her, decided that travelling was dangerous, and that she would not allow me to go alone. Much to my surprise, she said she would come with me. I was extremely grateful for her offer.

Mother went to look at our former apartment in Josefov, and there something quite unexpected occurred. Our neighbours returned a box of jewellery which they had hidden for us. Such honesty was not common. Miluška Hejzlarová, their daughter, had also kept safe my diary and the autograph book that Father had given me. Hesitantly, I asked Mother if we could take with us on our sad journey the gold ring with the red stone, the colour Violet dreamed of. Violet had never had a gold ring and I know how eagerly she hoped that the man she would one day marry would give her one. Mother instantly agreed.

We walked the few kilometres to the Jaroměř railway station. The timetable was unreliable and when a train did come it was crammed full. At last the train going to Železný Brod arrived. Willing hands pulled us through the window into the train. It was actually possible to sense how people had united. The sensation of being squashed in, unable to breathe, resembled the recent past, even though we were now travelling in an ordinary railway coach. But how much easier it was to tolerate the crush of bodies when it was voluntary and, above all, when you knew your destination! The train stopped often and we travelled for hours and hours. But I was not conscious of time. I thought about Jarmilka, my dear friend Violet, whose fate was so tragically tied to mine. She had been absolutely correct when she had written in one of her letters, 'It is good that we don't know what lies ahead ...'

Did we go to the slaughterhouse like sheep? Could everything have been different? Yes, we could have emigrated. As an experienced wine merchant, Father had had the promise of work in Australia, and a visa was assured. That was in 1938. But my parents had hesitated. Should we desert Grandma and Grandpa whom we might never see again?

Then our country was occupied by the force of specially trained troops of the SS and SA (*Sturmabteilung* – Storm Division). Could we have defended ourselves? I see my father in front of me, when he returned in 1938 from one of the border posts because his division had been demobilised. I remember how he cried.

And during the occupation? The inexorable progress of the Nazis, from small humiliations in everyday life to ultimate liquidation. They increased the number of measures towards the Jews step by step, by means of more and more edicts and ordinances. There was always the hope that it would be stopped at some stage. I remember conversations between my parents' friends when they hoped that world opinion, critical of persecution, would prevail. There was, also, the foolish belief that we lived in a progressive century. Fear and hope, hope and fear, that's how we lived and thought. Could we have defended ourselves against an ideology, fragmented as we were into individual families?

All this, and many other things, passed through my mind as the train carried me closer to Violet. The train jerked to a stop. We were pushed out of the carriage with the movement of the crowd and Mother and I looked around the small station. It was four years since I had met Violet, yet I was here for the first time. Mother and I – a lifetime older since the beginning of my friendship with Violet – took the road bordered by meadows. People willingly showed us the way, and it was obvious that the Holats were liked here.

About half an hour later, we reached the cottage which I had pictured from Violet's letters. There were geraniums in the window, and the branches of a lime-tree shaded the roof. On the paved area in front of the cottage were a bench and two cats, snuggled up in a ball. A shaggy mongrel yapped a welcome to us. Such tranquillity! The air was intoxicating in that first June of freedom. Surely it was not possible that suffering had no end? Why must my friend, my sister, die? Why now? My return to freedom seemed to have started badly.

From the photograph Violet had once shown me of her family I recognised the woman who now came out of the house. But what can one say to a mother whose daughter is dying? The three of us silently embraced. A girl came out of the cottage. Suddenly, a flash of hope – miracles sometimes happen and Violet believed in them so much. But it was her younger sister who looked so like her.

Mrs Holatová showed us in, and from the passage we climbed freshly scented, scrubbed wooden steps. I was already familiar with the little attic room, from Violet's letters. The sun's brilliance shone through the light curtains and almost blinded us. The two women paused, letting me go in alone. Violet saw nothing but me, and I nothing but her.

'Her eyes are full of life,' I thought to myself with renewed hope. If only the tubercular fever didn't burn her cheeks so!

'Tuberculosis is our family's illness, but it erupted with full force in prison,' I heard Violet's mother whisper to mine.

Violet's translucent hand hovered above the eiderdown and reached out to me. Meekly, I clasped her long, thin fingers and I had the feeling I was gripping something very fragile. I feel their pressure and then heard Violet whispering.

'I have lived to see you. Everything was worthwhile, yes, everything. If you had not returned ... but now you are here with me ... I am so happy that I have lived long enough ...'

I could not say anything. I reached into my pocket and opened the small box where, on red velvet, the ring of Violet's dreams lay. I put the ring on her thin finger. In her excitement she sat up so effortlessly that I was overwhelmed with hope. Violet did not know where to look first – at me, at her mother or at my mother. Then she looked again at the ring. She could not believe it. She, who had had no opportunity to experience a man's love, could feel such feminine joy when she received a small piece of jewellery, a token of love. All at once she began laughing, lightly, bell-like, then breathlessly. She held the red stone up to the sun. It glittered. Joyfully, we laughed with her. But not for long. Violet's laughter turned into a choking cough, and a stain, the colour of the stone, appeared on the pillow.

The fit of coughing exhausted her. She fell asleep and I sat by her until late into the night. From time to time she opened her eyes, gazed at me happily, then at the ring, and smiled. Towards morning, she died.

Mother and I didn't wait for the funeral. I didn't return with Mother to Josefov, but went directly to Prague so that, once again, I could go to the Repatriation Office. Again and again, a man came through the doors of the office and read out lists of names. Milan's was not among them, nor was my father's. Hope faded yet lingered on. I kept going back to that hallway and waiting, waiting.

These were my first weeks of freedom.

Afterwards

Seven years after the end of World War II, the shadow of those dismal Terezín buildings known as the Hamburg Barracks fell treacherously upon me once again.

I was due to sit postgraduate examinations in the Journalism Faculty of the University of Political and Social Science, Prague, at the end of June 1952. I had attended university for almost four years without having experienced many problems regarding my 'bourgeois' background. I endured the occasional criticism of friends who had working-class origins: that is, 'better' than mine. This was not particularly pleasant for me. At those times when they indicated that I was different, my fear, very familiar from the war years, surfaced.

In April, a few months before the final examinations, my anxiety intensified and I did not know why. The atmosphere around me became tense. During those years, which were, sadly, characterised by various political trials, the student committee of the Communist Party of Czechoslovakia ruled the University, and my friends were on it. These people, with whom I shared desks in lectures, were vigorously building the edifice of socialism in which they expected to live.

So I went to them and asked, 'What's going on, why are you avoiding me? Have I done something wrong?'

The first answer startled me. Apparently nothing was wrong, but in time I would know. What was I supposed to 'know'? And when would 'in time' be, if nothing had happened?

A friend from the student committee discreetly told me that a strange report about me had come from my home town, Josefov. She could not reveal what it contained.

Fourteen days elapsed before I was requested to attend the committee's proceedings. These were spent in painful soul-searching, seeking the slightest wrongdoing that I might have committed in Josefov. Finally, a report was read to me – I was not permitted to see it. The report stated that the National Committee in Josefov had not recommended that I should be allowed to sit for the examinations to complete my studies. Apparently, my mother had robbed the socialist state of half a million crowns. Furthermore, she had behaved in a 'bourgeois' manner and even had a car, which she drove wearing chamois gloves. And she wore slacks.

I was immediately able to explain the 'theft' of the money. Mother had borrowed money in 1946 to re-establish the family business, and the whole town could have easily ascertained that, by 1948, the debt had been repaid. But as soon as she had completed these transactions, her business, which had first been destroyed by the Nazis, was taken over by the Communists. For the second time in ten years my family had been dispossessed!

I expressed no opinion regarding the car, slacks and gloves because it all seemed absolutely ridiculous. So I asked, 'What is there to discuss? The loan was repaid, the state has lost nothing, the accusation is spurious.'

The answer, from those people I had lived with for almost four years, who had chatted with me every day and who knew me well, appalled me.

'We must believe the National Committee rather than you, as it is the representative of the people's government.'

Apparently they had already requested a more detailed explanation from the Josefov Committee. So I waited, through the weeks, for an answer, and the examination date drew closer. I requested that someone go with me to Josefov so that the whole matter could be settled more quickly. To this day, I am grateful that a fellow student, Daša, agreed to go with me. The accusations collapsed like a house of cards. No one from the National Committee claimed ownership of the illegible signature on the statement, and the answer to Daša's direct inquiry was, 'We have nothing against her.'

We returned to Prague, happy with the outcome. It finally seemed that my graduation would depend solely on my knowledge and not on false statements. But at the last moment, the Hamburg Barracks was to emerge. The atmosphere around me did not clear after the visit to Josefov. On the contrary, it grew murkier. Following the first statement from Josefov, there had been only furtive looks from some of my 'better-informed' fellow students, but now some of them began, noticeably, to avoid me, while others rather conspiratorially gave the impression that they sympathised with me.

The student committee convened again, and now informed me that they had received a letter from the personnel office of the University with evidence that I had not liberated myself from my bourgeois origins. Once again I was perplexed and searched for the nature of my wrongdoing. The questions put to me were not direct, yet it was somehow up to me to say what and when I had done wrong, say that I admitted and regretted it. 'Surely, I must know this?'

Those who have not experienced the agony of having a confession extorted for something they have never done cannot understand the gravity of such a situation. The worst thing was that I had no idea what it was about. Although I had pondered all my past actions and even my past thoughts, I found nothing for which I could be accused. Something had been investigated and I did not know what. At that time, I was not familiar with Franz Kafka's *The Castle* and *The Trial*, although I was living their characters' experiences.

I was called up before the committee in Chancellor Ladislav Štoll's office. The committee had to decide what would happen to me. It did not look good. Apart from the Chancellor, the University Secretary and the chairwoman of the Students' Communist Party Committee sat at the table.

'How would you define your attitude to us, your attitude as a student of journalism in this era of building socialism? How can you justify what has happened?'

'What actually has happened?'

Eventually, they told me. An airmail letter addressed to me was produced from among the papers on the Chancellor's desk. It was a letter which I had left in a book borrowed from the Faculty library two years before. When the librarian recently found it, she did not return it to me but, convinced that she was carrying out her duty, she handed it to the Faculty personnel office. From there it travelled to the Chancellor and the campaign began.

So at last I knew what was going on. It was a letter from Milan. Miraculously, Milan had returned from the concentration camp. However, he had not returned to me. After the death march, my shining hero was a different person. The glow had evaporated. The war, that had destroyed everything, also shattered very deep feelings. Milan had emigrated, but from the threads of our relationship an unbreakable strand remained. We had even corresponded after February 1948, when it was not very safe to write to emigrants.

That letter had been Milan's last one, a message from an exotic country, Chile. It was the last, because by losing the letter I had also lost his address. I knew by heart the letter that was now lying in front of the Chancellor. I could have repeated its contents practically word for word, even after those two long years. When I looked at it again, it struck me in a flash that what Milan had written so flippantly and cynically would not be taken lightly by the leadership of the University.

'Rečík,' Milan had written, 'I am married and have two children. Perhaps you'll be surprised but I often think about you. My life was pretty adventurous after crossing the border in 1948, but finally I have found a country which is furthest from the east and from all that happened there. From my father I have probably inherited the philosophy which he formulated: "money is lying in the streets, you only need to bend down and pick it up". I have tried all sorts of things and now, I don't know how long it will last, a business partner and I have a small factory for liqueurs and a wine shop. As far as I remember, your father had something similar and your mother began production again after returning from the concentration camp. I could use her here now because I don't understand it a bit. Probably the drinks we produce are not much good, but they sell. You know, ordinary people guzzle anything.'

The room was quiet and the eyes of the three judges followed me closely, as I pretended to read the letter again, this time through their eyes. I realised that it was an appalling mess – a close friendship with someone who is a capitalist and also cynical about 'the people'. Suddenly, the last sentences from the letter leapt out:

'Remember, Rečík, our last night in the Hamburg Barracks? The night we spent awake on the straw mattress? I will never forget that giddy time!

'Your life has gone on along a different path from mine. I simply could not stay in Europe where my brother, my parents and my whole family perished. I will never forget you and I will be happy if you write.

'Your Milan.'

In a silence which seemed endless, my thoughts were spinning. What will they do with me? A few days ago the statement from Josefov, and now this. In those years, a lesser offence was quite enough for suspicion and subsequent conviction.

The voice of one of the committee members broke the silence.

'How can you explain that you were in barracks in Hamburg and with someone for the whole night in a state of giddiness on a straw mattress? It must have been an American soldier or officer. How and when did you go there?'

It was a bad dream. This could not be real. I had the impulsive desire to stand up and leave. If the opportunity to finish my first university degree had not depended on the outcome, I would certainly have done so.

Haltingly, I explained: the transports, Milan, the Hamburg Barracks, and that last night with Milan in the Terezín ghetto.

A different silence pervaded the room. They had not counted on this explanation. Obviously such things had not occurred to them. Finally, the Chancellor said, 'Perhaps it is as you say. Let the committee for your year conclude the investigation now and close the whole case. I entrust the decision of what to do with you to the committee.'

All at once it seemed better than could have been expected. There were people on the students' committee of the Czech Communist Party who liked me (at least that is what I thought) and who would believe me. They listened attentively and ultimately decided: we believe you but comrade Chancellor is completely disgusted by the amoral tone of this letter and he would rather not see you at the University. Write a description of the whole episode and explain how you met this person, Milan, and justify how such a person could be an intimate. If you are convincing, then we will support you and you can complete your studies.

I did it. In that false confession I stated that if I had known what Milan was really like, I could not possibly have loved him.

It must have been convincing because I was not expelled. I completed my university studies on the basis of a lie which I had written. The memory of this still humiliates me. It finally seemed, however, that the story of the Hamburg Barracks had come to an end.

And yet ... Twenty years had elapsed since my graduation from university when, in 1974, my adolescent daughter Lenka and I applied for a permit to travel to England via Paris. Permits were required to travel anywhere beyond the socialist bloc. Usually this involved standing in a long queue at the police office, then an anxious wait to see whether the request would be accepted. After a few weeks, final permission would be received. I waited in the long queue in front of the police office and received then some incredible news. 'Your daughter has permission, but you have not. You will receive a letter of notification from the Ministry of Interior.' Once again I had to endure the feeling of powerlessness, of being a marked person about whom someone, somewhere, made decisions without having to justify them. Nor was there any possibility of appealing for justice. The printed words 'It is not in the Republic's interest' leapt out from that 'explanatory' letter. Telling myself that I was not the only person rejected did not console me. I lodged an appeal but it was dismissed immediately and I was informed that the decision was final. I could not protest again.

Why could Lenka, a minor, go and not I? Possibly they assumed that I would not allow her to go alone. If they thought like that, they had miscalculated. I wanted her to see the world and so she went on her own. But what could they have against me?

Once again, I examined my life. Apart from common misdemeanours such as any ordinary person committed – writing to friends abroad, making friends with an Australian woman studying in Prague, occasionally attending a film at the American Embassy – there was nothing else I could think of.

Apparently one of our colleagues at work had contacts within the Secret Police. They said that about many people in Czechoslovakia, but I wondered if it were true. I told him the details of the permit refusal and, strangely enough, without hesitating he answered, 'I'll have a look at it, I know some of "the boys".'

A few weeks later, with a sly expression, he said to me, 'You have some very unpleasant things from the past in your dossier. If you want me to help you, you must tell me the truth!'

'But about what? I have no idea what it could be. Can't you at least indicate what it's all about?'

'Where were you immediately after the war, when you returned from the ghetto?' Eventually he blurted this out and it was clear that the question embarrassed him.

'It's very simple,' I said. 'From Terezín I went to Josefov, then for three years I was in Mělník where I went to school and matriculated, and then Prague and the journalism faculty ...'

'No, that's not it, you are omitting something. Go back to 1945,

straight after the war. Does Hamburg mean something to you: West
Germany, American soldiers?'
   'No, I have never been to West Germany. Out of the question!'
   'Well,' said my colleague who knew 'the boys', it's all in your dossier. Quite distinctly. 'Hamburg, barracks, a mattress, an American
soldier or perhaps an officer? Think back ...'
   As he rattled this off, it clicked. I had already explained everything
about Milan's letter, which had almost disqualified me from complet-
ing my degree. It was more than twenty years since I had had to make
that degrading statement. But they did not destroy that letter and the
Chancellor had obviously passed it on. My file must be in the Ministry of Interior and the letter with it.
   Once again, I had to explain, only now it was to my colleague. He
believed me. The solution to my problem, however, was not so simple.
   'I cannot arrange the removal of that letter from your dossier,' he
said. 'I'm glad I have put you on the right track, but now only someone
in State Security can help you.'
   It was better than knowing nothing, but how much better?
   For years I had tried to live inconspicuously and not get mixed up in
anything. I wanted my daughter to be able to study in peace. But should
I let this business lie? Obviously, I would never be able to visit countries beyond the socialist border and I would always feel imprisoned.
   I decided not to hurry but that if I met someone who could help me, I
would not turn the offer down. The chance came in the person of a young
secretary at the Socialist Academy, where I had been lecturing in philosophy for some years. I do not even remember how we came to discuss my
travel problems. The young woman reacted quite spontaneously.
   'Here is the phone number of a man who can certainly help,' she
said, and she described to me a very fine man.
   He was a major in the Secret Police. He suggested a meeting in a café
in Wenceslas Square. I went there and once again told my story about the
Hamburg Barracks in Terezín. After an hour-long discussion he gave me
a telephone number and told me I should call him in two weeks.
   After that call, it was the same café and the same table, and further
discussion of the same subject. After the third meeting, he informed
me that things were going well and he asked me to collaborate with
the Secret Police. He immediately added, however, that even if I didn't
agree, my case would be satisfactorily resolved.
   I remember what I said as if it were today. I had anticipated that, in

return for the freedom to travel, I would have to become an informer. My response had been prepared beforehand.

'I have been held in a concentration camp, I long for neither money nor high social standing, and my daughter has emigrated. I am not interested in cooperating with the police and I have no idea why the Secret Police would have any interest in me ...'

'Very well,' he said, 'forget my question, forget about our meetings and do not speak to anyone about this. Next time you apply for permission to travel, it will be in order.'

The major had not lied. Next time it was indeed all right. After two years of groping in the dark and feeling insecure it was possible to breathe more easily.

After returning from several trips abroad, I thought about the man who had helped me gain that freedom. I wanted to thank him and I rang the number he had given me. A strange voice answered with a typically impersonal response and I asked for the major's number. The voice at the other end of the line asked sharply, 'Who is calling?'

I replaced the receiver. Who knows where he had disappeared to? I heard nothing more about him and I considered the case of the Hamburg Barracks finished for ever.

But when information is placed in one's police file, it usually has a very long life, as long, indeed, as the regime itself.

So again ... Only one of my cousins returned from the concentration camps. Her maiden name, too, was Friesová. Erna was an agricultural engineer and for years she worked on documentary films dealing with agricultural subjects. In the 1970s, after the Soviet occupation, purges began in the film industry. Erna was summoned to the committee evaluating personal credentials and, 'for serious reasons which cannot be divulged', was dismissed from the industry. After that, she worked as a tractor driver.

Naturally, she wanted to know the reasons which had led to her dismissal and condemned her to manual labour. She searched until she discovered the reasons. Apparently a report had been sent from the Ministry of Interior to her workplace alleging that, after the war, she had been in Hamburg and had had an affair with an American soldier. She had no idea what this was all about. She defended herself; she argued; she searched futilely for the basis of these absurd accusations. Her protests met an impenetrable wall.

Later, we met in the Monastery Restaurant in Prague and discussed all that had happened in those years since the war. I mentioned the story of Milan's letter which nearly prevented me from graduating and which, years later, was also the reason for the ban on my travelling outside the republic. When I told her about the absurd connection of the Hamburg Barracks and the giddiness of young love, I felt Erna's eyes boring into me. She didn't interrupt my story, but when I had finished she exploded: 'I sensed that my fate was somehow closely connected with yours. Indeed, our names are so similar, I suspected as much, but I had no one to tell. They would not speak to me, they didn't believe a word I said. That is why I had to leave the film industry and wander from one state farm to another as a tractor driver, in order just to live.'

I froze. It was unbelievable. A solitary lost letter which the librarian had failed to return to me but, instead, had passed on to the university Chancellor, had blighted not only my life but my cousin Erna's too. I sat in front of her like a criminal and, completely bewildered, apologised.

After all these years, the Hamburg Barracks still evoked fear in my heart. Even though the activities in the barracks had been directed by the Nazi regime, the subsequent regime, and its state security Secret Police, had branded two people's lives with fear and loss.

And now for the last of the Hamburg Barracks. After fifty years, Milan returned from Chile to visit Prague, the city of his birth. We met and spoke about our children and grandchildren, and about our lives. The conversation drifted to the Hamburg Barracks and that final night that we had spent together.

'Were you surprised that I didn't answer your first (and last) letter from Santiago?' I asked, and told him the story of the letter.

He was stunned. 'I will never forgive myself for the problems I caused because of that letter. Can you ever forgive me?'

But there was – is – nothing to forgive. The saga of the Hamburg Barracks is not only a testimony of the times but it is also about puritanism, suspicion, cowardice and repression. They all thrive in the soil of any totalitarian regime.